COMMUNICATION
WITH
All Life

HAY HOUSE TITLES OF RELATED INTEREST

YOU CAN HEAL YOUR LIFE, the movie, starring Louise Hay
& Friends (available as a 1-DVD program and an expanded 2-DVD set)
Watch the trailer at: **www.LouiseHayMovie.com**

❖ ❖

*ANIMALS AND THE AFTERLIFE: True Stories
of Our Best Friends' Journey Beyond Death,*
by Kim Sheridan

*ANIMAL SPIRIT GUIDES: An Easy-to-Use Handbook for Identifying
Your Power Animals and Animal Spirit Helpers,*
by Steven D. Farmer, Ph.D.

*CHAKRA CLEARING: Awakening Your Spiritual Power
to Know and Heal,* by Doreen Virtue (book-with-CD)

*FOLLOWING SOUND INTO SILENCE: Chanting Your Way Beyond
Ego into Bliss,* by Kurt (Kailash) A. Bruder, Ph.D., M.Ed.
(book-with-CD)

*THE LAW OF ATTRACTION: The Basics of the
Teachings of Abraham*™, by Esther and Jerry Hicks

*MARK'S POWER PEEK 2008: A Daily
Astrological Companion,* by Mark S. Husson

NATURAL HEALING FOR DOGS AND CATS A–Z,
by Cheryl Schwartz, D.V.M.

*NATURAL NUTRITION FOR CATS:
The Path to Purr-fect Health,*
*NATURAL NUTRITION FOR DOGS AND CATS:
The Ultimate Diet,* and
*THE NATURAL NUTRITION NO-COOK BOOK:
Delicious Food for You . . . and Your Pets,*
all by Kymythy R. Schultze

*WHAT TO DO WHEN YOU DON'T KNOW WHAT TO DO:
Common Horse Sense,* by Wyatt Webb

All of the above are available at your local
bookstore, or may be ordered by visiting:

Hay House USA: **www.hayhouse.com**®
Hay House Australia: **www.hayhouse.com.au**
Hay House UK: **www.hayhouse.co.uk**
Hay House India: **www.hayhouse.co.in**

COMMUNICATION
WITH
All Life

REVELATIONS OF AN
ANIMAL COMMUNICATOR

JOAN RANQUET

HAY HOUSE, INC.
Carlsbad, California • New York City
London • Sydney • New Delhi

Published in the United States by: Hay House, Inc.: www.hayhouse.com
Published in Australia by: Hay House Australia Pty. Ltd.: www.hayhouse.com.au
Published in the United Kingdom by: Hay House UK, Ltd.: www.hayhouse.co.uk
Published in India by: Hay House Publishers India: www.hayhouse.co.in

Design: Tricia Breidenthal
Photos courtesy of the author

Library of Congress Cataloging-in-Publication Data

Ranquet, Joan.
  Communication with all life : revelations of an animal communicator / Joan Ranquet.
    p. cm.
  ISBN 978-1-4019-1681-7 (tradepaper)
  1. Pets--Behavior--Anecdotes. 2. Animals--Behavior--Anecdotes. 3. Human-animal communication--Anecdotes. 4. Communication--Psychological aspects. 5. Telepathy--Anecdotes. 6. Ranquet, Joan. 7. Animal communicators--Anecdotes. I. Title.
  SF412.5.R36 2007
  636.088'7--dc22   2007009837

ISBN: 978-1-4019-1681-7

1st edition, November 2007
2nd edition, January 2008
1st digital printing, January 2016

Printed in the United States of America

❖ ❖

This book is dedicated to
both of my amazing parents.
My mother woke up out of a coma
on her deathbed and told me,
"Joan, you have lost a book."
Here it is, Mom.

❖ ❖

Please Note: All of the stories and case studies in this book are true; however, some names have been changed for confidentiality purposes.

❖ Contents ❖

❖ Preface ❖

There once was a little girl who was so obsessed with horses that *horse* was the first word out of her mouth. She had her mother drive by pastures where the animals were grazing just to see them. When she was old enough to ride a bike, she would pedal the long way home to watch them run, see their manes and tails blowing in the breeze, and breathe in their smells. Their thundering hooves made her heart pound.

When the little girl was seven, her mother took her to a horse show. She watched every event with awe. At a break, they announced that a horse would be raffled off. The little girl told her mother that it was *hers*. The mother informed her that, yes, they'd bought five tickets, but these were merely chances to win; it wasn't "her" horse. "Oh no, that's my horse," the little girl insisted.

While playing in the backyard with friends after the show, the little girl announced that she'd won a horse. "No way," her friends all said. But they couldn't rain on her parade . . . she knew better.

When the phone rang that evening, she was sure that it was about her horse. She heard her father repeating, "No, I can't believe it!" He was laughing and even cussing: She had never heard her father swear before.

When he got off the phone, he confirmed that she had, indeed, won the horse, who was moved to a barn in the neighborhood.

Now she could ride her bike to visit her *own* horse. She learned all about grooming and equipment. Even though her new pet was an untrained two-year-old, he treated her carefully and lovingly. He took her on his back through trails, and together they learned many things about the basics of riding in an arena. She *loved* this horse and he loved her.

Nevertheless, her parents feared that he was too much for a young girl. After all, he was a quarter horse, descended from a famous racehorse. He would need further training, and it would be more appropriate for her if they were to get a different kind of horse—a safer one—later on. They arranged to sell the horse and put the money in their daughter's bank account.

The little girl was devastated. When she stood in the bank with people explaining savings and interest, she was aware that their lips were moving, but she heard nothing. She was standing on a rug now instead of in the sawdust shavings. There were no good smells. There was nothing.

In the hopes that she'd get over her disappointment, her parents promised that if she learned more, she could eventually get another horse. In the meantime, she got a puppy named Penny. After a couple of years working at a local Arabian-horse farm, where she continued her lessons, the little girl's parents kept their word and bought her another horse.

Her love of these animals never abated, and years later she attended a riding camp, where she saw a horse that looked like her first one. When he spotted her, he went crazy in his pen, neighing loudly to get her attention. She asked a groom what the horse's name was, and it turned out, indeed, to be her old companion. They got to meet once again.

That little girl was me, and the horse was Hanky Panky. That one chance pulled out of a hat in a raffle ushered in a lifetime of horses, other animals, and love: one where very little else matters nearly as much as those things. Living in that world of silent communication with another creature, sharing love and being brought to laughter, holds more currency for me than anything else.

— Joan Ranquet

❖ Introduction ❖

Some of my best leading men
have been dogs and horses.
— Elizabeth Taylor

I always joke that I haven't really changed since the age of seven when some neighborhood friends and I started a club, for which I still have the bylaws. We were all good Catholic girls—but also witches who could perform magic. (Yes, *Mary Poppins* is still my favorite movie because she's the only female metaphysical hero I know.) We were obsessed with horses, as are many girls. The intention of our club was to buy one by performing plays that I'd written and then selling the script after the show.

That was the year I won my first horse, Hanky Panky, and the world was spared my plays written out with bad penmanship. (Not a single relative could avoid my performances at holidays, however.) The four themes of writing, performing, horses, and some form of mystical/spirit-driven adventure that permeated my childhood have remained driving forces throughout my entire life.

Hanky Panky was just the beginning of the equine adventure. My sisters also became horse obsessed. Rather than paying board for many animals, my parents bought five acres in a suburb outside of Seattle, where I grew up. At one point between the three of us, we had ten horses. My father wasn't always aware of just how many my mother bought!

Lessons in Horse Sense

My connection to horses continued even when I went to Stephens College in Columbia, Missouri, and received a degree in theater. While there, I joined the Prince of Wales Club, one of the oldest continually active riding teams in the country.

Still, dramatic arts took over as the winner of the four dominating themes in my life, and upon graduation, I went to New York City to pursue my dream of acting. And, of course, I wandered through the horse barns in Central Park regularly. I could have overdosed on the excitement of my New York life.

Then a phone call came informing me that my sister Laurie had been diagnosed with a stage-four cancerous brain tumor. In shock, I went to the NYU alternative-health library and read up on healing options. As I headed back to Seattle, my luggage contained the beginning of my putting the mystical part of the four themes in my life to work. I believed in my heart of hearts that God's will permitting, a healing could occur for Laurie.

At home, in my naïveté, I spouted off about visualization, about figuring out how to move the bad cells out of the way. "Let's talk to the cancer," I told my sister. The piles of books that I trotted out were left collecting dust. While I was the oldest of four, I was suddenly treated like the baby (maybe even delusional) sister for having such grandiose ideas and for what everyone else believed was denial. I was incredulous at the idea that my entire family had surrendered, dropped their faith, and handed over such almighty power to one doctor who said that my sister was going to die.

Despite my expecting a miracle, Laurie died in December 1986, ten days shy of her 22nd birthday.

I remained in Seattle for a year navigating through epic grief. An avid reader, I constantly searched, seeking out answers. I still believed in miracles, and I knew that I had to come to terms with the death of Laurie's hopes, dreams, and spirit.

When I was ready to move on, I decided to go to the entertainment-industry mecca itself, Los Angeles. One of the first things I packed was all of my horse gear: a jumping saddle, a Western saddle, bridles, boots, riding pants, and chaps. Just as when I was a child, I *knew* that I was getting a horse.

Working in theater in Los Angeles brought me into contact with an extraordinary number of gay men, and they were dying off in droves from AIDS. I found myself once again sitting bedside, but now for very sick young men. The loss of these talents was beyond tragic. As I watched their bodies and spirits just withering away, I sought meaning. I honestly thought that I was there to help them because I had walked through the experience with Laurie. That was the gift that came from her death.

One of the young men, Barry, had a horse called Kubla that he was too ill to care for. So I did it for him. Then Kubla died of colic. It was as if he were loaning his Barry a little more time and would be there waiting for him when he crossed.

With sadness, I went to the barn to get my equipment. Just as I arrived, the barn manager, Elaine, turned a horse out in the arena. She was the most stunning one I'd ever seen: dark brown—nearly black—an exotic beauty with an ebony mane and tail and a little white star on her face. She put on a show for me, running and bucking and hurling her big spirit around. Her name was Pet One, and she was for sale.

At the time I was very invested in my starving-artist routine. How could I afford a horse? Amazingly, an unsolicited credit card arrived in the mail that very day, and I used the money as a deposit on her. Horse people know that the purchase price is just the beginning. The real cost is the care, the shoes, the lessons, and the equipment. And every month, miraculously, I paid for it—although sometimes barely. Pet One made everything worth living for.

If there were ever a soul mate in animal form, Pet One was it: She was me in a horse suit! She was funny, very social, and affectionate with me—and like me, she had a wild streak. When I rode her, we were a unit; we were no longer separate species, but one.

My horse/soul needs were being met by riding and caring for Pet One. I also explored energy classes and lectures, meditation methods, Mass, yoga, Alexander Technique, moon dances, flamenco (okay, that wasn't really spiritual, just fun!), and sweat lodges. In my horse, I had such a big spirit-activating hobby that it was almost a challenge to continue studying acting, let alone do some dumb job.

Around this time, Elaine invited Lydia Hibby, a well-known animal communicator, to the barn to have our horses "talked to" or "heard." I was intrigued. Around the time of my sister's death, I learned to read tarot cards, but this was a different reading of energy: Lydia was really *talking* to the horse. She expressed how strongly Pet One and I loved each other. I felt very close to Pet One after the experience. It confirmed a lot of the depth of feeling I had for her, as well as many of the things that I seemed to intuitively know about the other horses in the barn.

Great Expectations

Pet One was offered a breeding, and I thought that it was a fantastic idea. Once she was pregnant, I found myself eating in restaurants alone, absorbing every word of books on foaling and preparing for the big day. I sensed that Pet One really wanted me there for the birth. Close to midnight on May 9, I was about to leave the barn when Solomon, the deaf and mute Mexican groom, gestured in one of his typically excited pantomimes that the moon was just right and I should stay. I pulled my car into the barn aisle right next to the opening to Pet One's feed tub and slept with my window rolled down.

At about 3 A.M., I woke to the noise of Pet One's water breaking, and I knew that a baby would be out in 20 minutes if everything went right. I woke up Elaine and her daughter, Patty, and then ran back to the stall to coach, breathe, and do whatever it took to ensure a perfect birth. Twenty minutes passed; there was no baby. We realized that a hoof seemed to be coming out of Pet One's anus. While we waited for the vet, Patty and I had to go inside Pet One during contractions to redirect the hooves and try to bring the foal on down through the birth canal. Our efforts worked: Somewhere around 4 A.M. the cutest foal was born . . . a little chocolate drop of a guy, absolute perfection. He was a bay, brown with a black mane and tail and a star on his forehead that was as bright as the light on a miner's hat. I put my hands all over him to imprint him to accept me as well as his mother as an important part of his life. It was truly one of the happiest moments of my life.

And when I say "moments," I really mean it, as I'd lain down on the couch for not even a minute after arriving home in the afternoon when the phone rang: Elaine was horrified—Pet One was in the throes of colic.

I made what was normally a 45-minute drive through traffic in 14 minutes. When I got there, Elaine was walking—more like dragging—a weak, sweat-drenched Pet One to keep her from rolling on the ground and twisting her gut completely. Horses can't throw up, so when they have extreme indigestion, their delicate intestinal system can twist and kill them. The baby was screaming and desperately trying to nurse. When my vet arrived, he recommended immediate surgery.

Surgery would be in Chino, about an hour away on a good day, and we were looking at rush-hour traffic. If a horse does have a twisted gut, generally you have one hour before tissue dies and then so does the animal. We loaded Pet One and the baby into a borrowed trailer. Solomon rode in it with the horses. I followed in my car, praying the whole way.

When we arrived at the hospital, Pet One's big 17-hand-tall body was sprawled out in the horse trailer. Solomon's face was white. After years of seeing me at the barn, he—more than anyone—knew how much Pet One's life and my own completely revolved around each other.

The vet came out, and even though Pet One still had a pulse, he suggested euthanizing her right there in the trailer.

I came unglued. "Try. Just fix her!" I screamed—that's the cleaned-up version. In truth, there were some swear words involved. They took Pet One into surgery immediately.

The baby was unwieldy and bouncing around. Nourishment for infant horses must be available on a continual basis, and they usually don't go more than an hour without nursing. We could barely control him. I was terror stricken. I stayed in a stall with him, sobbing, hoping that someone could find goat milk; otherwise, I could potentially lose both of them. I realized that the foal might never be with his mother again. And since he would quite possibly end up with a human mom, I named him Pony Boy.

During those dark hours, I wondered whether Pony Boy had gotten enough colostrum from his mother's milk within the first 12 hours to build his immune antibodies. I agonized about whether giving Pet One a warm bran mash right after the birth had sent her stomach into hell. I questioned everything.

Pet One did survive a 360-degree twist of the intestine and a very complicated and harsh surgery. Only time would tell if it was to be successful.

During the next five weeks, sleep became something I just dreamed of. I lived at the barn in L.A., setting an alarm to replenish Pony Boy's supply of goat milk every hour. And every day I trekked to Chino to see Pet One. She was so inside herself trying to find the place to recover. I put my hands on her where I knew the most damage had been and rested against her.

I had to find an alternative situation for Pony Boy. I contacted vets all over the area to find out if there was another orphan colt that he could be with or a mare that had lost a foal and would take Pony Boy. Nothing. My sister Mary came from Seattle to help. Everyone I knew stopped in to see the little foal or even hold the bottle for him. His stall became a meeting place. There were charts for everything: Pony Boy's goat-milk feeding, foal formula, medication, and poop schedule.

Five weeks later, Pet One eventually came home. I stopped sleeping at the barn then. After more than a month of hearing distant freight trains and feeling the wind come off the Los Angeles River at night, I returned to urban living. No longer was I greeted by the horses' sleepy-eyed, loving nature. Now as I looked into apartments and houses, it was odd to see people in the windows.

One day I walked Pet One over to Pony Boy's stall. Pony Boy desperately tried to connect with his mother, calling out to her. Sadly, she was very remote . . . she still really needed every ounce of her energy to stay alive. It became obvious that mother and baby would never be together again. And that was the last time—ever—that Pony Boy tried to bond with a horse.

Two weeks later, Pet One suffered another bout of colic. This time her colon had flipped and her entire system was full of adhesions from the first surgery. The surgeon actually said that all the places he had seen me lay my hands were fine, but that the rest of the tissue was dead.

I had no choice but to let her go. I zoomed back on the freeway as if I couldn't flee from the pain fast enough. At one point I was so hysterical and screaming so loudly that I had to pull over. I'd never feel her stride again. I'd never again hear her little low-grumble "hello."

There are still no words to describe the loss of Pet One.

Pony Boy: A Lost Soul

Even though I was shattered, I had an orphan colt to care for. It was heartbreaking—and unnatural—to see the adorable, two-month-old foal in a big stall by himself: He got more attention than anyone should. And, oh, was he smart. There was a pay phone outside of his stall that I used a lot. When he walked out, he would pick up the receiver! I realized that this was a case of monkey see, monkey do, entirely based on my behavior. So when it came time to teach him to eat hay—you guessed it. . . .

As he matured, he began exhibiting young stud-colt behavior. A mother would turn or kick out if her offspring tried to mount her. The only thing a young stud *respected* was his mother, and he would learn his manners from her. I couldn't do that. I started carrying a large metal garbage-can top, which I called the magical shield. His hooves hitting it would surprise him, which more or less ended that behavior.

Having once been prey, horses have a built-in fight-or-flight mechanism, just like humans. Additionally, they understand and comply with herd behavior. Pony Boy didn't have any of that instinct; he had no horse traits. His anger would mount toward others if they didn't pay attention to him as they had when he was a cute little foal they could hug like a puppy. He and I could sit in another world and just be. However, with other people, he would lunge violently and bite. And then his eyes would soften as if to say, "I'm sorry—I just want your love."

Even after he was gelded, this dominant behavior continued. I was making plans to get him into a setting with other horses where he could learn to be one of them when I noticed that he wasn't putting down his left hind leg. X-rays revealed that he had osteochondritis dissecans (OCD), which means a death of a portion of the bone, joint, or cartilage. His bones looked like Swiss cheese as a result of not getting enough mineral intake from his mother and receiving too much protein in the foal formula.

My options were to euthanize Pony Boy, which is what many breeders would do in a case this severe, or make dietary changes. Having lost his mother, I chose to keep him alive. He needed to be confined in small enclosures so as not to shatter the barely attached bone and also to get less protein.

For months I went along with the vet's plan for Pony Boy's OCD, but also continued with my own program. I did everything from praying, to visualizing Pony Boy's bones as perfect. I performed energy work on his legs, massaging them to bring more circulation to the area. I even lit candles for him at St. Victor's Church in West Hollywood and worked with a Lakota Sioux man named Butch Artichoker, who had a sweat-lodge ceremony for Pony Boy in South Dakota. I followed Butch's instructions and walked Pony Boy to the Los Angeles River at midnight under the full moon and broke a gourd over his back.

Six months later, Pony Boy's bones were perfect. In fact, the vet accused me of swapping out x-rays. I told him the whole list of things I'd done. He laughed—he'd always been amused by my methods.

Pony Boy could now go out to pasture. I decided to board him in a mountain town an hour and a half north of L.A. so that he could be "weaned" from me. I'd just go up twice a week. On one visit, we hiked to the top of a mountain, and I thought, *What if I just slipped onto his back?* He was a little over two years old. In a perfect world, I would have waited until he was about three before I rode him, but I was running out of ideas to entertain him. We had done some groundwork; I felt that he was just waiting for me to hop on. So I climbed astride him. He just stood there . . . it was the most peaceful moment I've ever had. And then as though someone were speaking right into my ear, I clearly heard the words *I've been waiting for this.* I had to look around to make sure that someone wasn't talking, but there was no other human for miles and miles. We just stayed there a while taking in the view of the valley.

But the grim reports started coming. Pony Boy's aggression led people to call him "evil." Inevitably, he was evicted.

I arranged for him to go to Seattle for training with my sister, but matters didn't improve, and before long Pony Boy had pretty much attacked everyone there, too. We even tried a "horse whisperer," a trainer who uses methods based on the equine psychology and horses' natural herd behavior. But it was more of the same. Nobody could safely get near Pony Boy's stall.

I flew up to see him, and at first he seemed his normal self. Then I turned to leave the stall and felt a huge thud from a hoof in the middle of my back. I was knocked to the ground. In all my years of being with horses, I'd never been scared, but now I was. It's got to be one of the worst feelings on the planet, being terrified of someone you've loved, raised, and trusted. The next day he struck out at me again, nailing me in the shoulder. Now I was beside myself. I loved Pony Boy, but the situation was very bleak.

I was beyond bereft. Here I'd lost his mother, and now the horse I'd raised as my own terrified me. He was a criminal, a walking lawsuit. He was so angry that there was no turning him around.

In the wild, he and Pet One would have died at the time of his birth. If he had survived, it wouldn't have been for long. Anyone else would have put him down when the severity of the OCD was revealed. Perhaps the kindest thing to do was to was to let him go . . . to hit the restart button on his karma and allow him some peace and a chance to begin anew. And that's what I did.

Studying Animal Communication

When Pony Boy was less than a year old, there was another boarder at the barn who had no time for his mare, Gabrielle. She was a striking little bay Arab: golden brown with a very long black mane and tail. Although she had little training, she had fancy bloodlines, and her owner could have asked a pretty penny for her. Instead, he simply handed me the papers! She is, to this day, a stunning mare.

In my despondent state after losing Pony Boy, Gabrielle was my one ray of hope. However, she developed a mysterious lameness, and x-rays didn't shed light on the root of the problem. I wanted to consult the animal communicator Lydia Hibby about it but couldn't find her phone number. Then one day I saw a class advertised with another well-known expert, Carol Gurney. So off I went.

The animal-communication class was not only fun, but it also confirmed for me that I did indeed have this ability. Getting quiet and entering the silent world to tune in to animals also reconnected me with the labyrinth of coexistence that I felt when I ripped through the woods bareback on my beloved Honeyhorse in my teens. Still, I harbored a healthy skepticism, and at a cellular level I'm a huge smart-ass! In fact, if you had told me then that this would be my life path, I'd have thought you were crazy. I was under the impression that I was only taking the class for my own needs and amusement.

I even went into Carol's professional program, still asserting that it was simply to deepen my connection with my own animals. Here's where everything I'd learned in all the years of energy classes came together. Having meditated for so long gave me a huge leg up throughout the whole process. I could navigate my own internal chatter and really hear or see what was being expressed to me by a nonverbal being. All the years of studying, acting, and writing gave me the ability to dissect a story that an animal told me and separate it from what the human was telling me—which enabled me to objectively take the situation or the dynamic apart and put the pieces back together in such a way that the person could understand the animal's behavior and make an adjustment in the household.

I had a breakthrough one day when I asked my friend's horse, Flash, if he wanted to learn to jump. I heard *Yippee!* in the same way I'd heard Pony Boy speak to me. Flash was a stellar student, and it was as if he'd been waiting for this moment. Perhaps he'd been sending us the message all along and we were just now responding to it.

Around that time, I also learned TTouch, a type of healing massage created first for horses, then for companion animals, by Linda Tellington-Jones. I learned an energetic-healing technique called the Bioscalar Wave, which redistributes the energy in the body's electromagnetic field to correct disease. Gabrielle was receptive to it, and in due course, I was able to manage her lameness—which turned out to be a vaccine-related nervous-system breakdown.

Uniting My Passions

I still had writing jobs, but increasingly people wanted me to help them with their pets. Telling folks in L.A. that you're doing this work is like lighting hay on fire—word spreads fast. As I look back on the city, good and bad, one thing is certain: It's an energy-work gymnasium, and I was "exercising" regularly.

I became very busy practicing my new hobby. I drove around to the homes or barns of people I didn't even know, sitting down, getting quiet, and connecting with their animals. I would write down all the impressions of what they told me through feelings, words, and pictures and then express them to the person. Through my knowledge of human behavior (from studying acting for years) as well as that of animals (by practically living in a stall), I was able to come up with reasonable suggestions to rectify most problems or give referrals to professionals who could. I found the names of great dog trainers, holistic vets, and equine or canine massage therapists whom I could recommend.

I had to start charging gas money as the volume of consultations grew. Eventually, I had to admit to myself that this was a full-time occupation. I was forced to release the acting and screenwriting dreams and totally immerse myself in my new life. The stories I tapped into within the walls of every home I visited were way more compelling than anything I could have created at the computer.

As both a writer and an actress, I was primarily drawn to comedy, and I truly believe that nothing is worth doing if you can't get a good laugh out of it! Through humor, I can defuse a situation so that people don't feel so guilty or bad about it and can make a healthy attempt at setting things right, whether it's a human/animal problem or an animal/animal one. The other remarkable thing that happened in making this lifestyle and career change was that unlike when I was an actress, I was in demand! I've always joked that I finally got a steady job when I became a pet psychic.

In the end, as much as I've studied this work and as many classes as I take, Pet One and Pony Boy were not just great teachers . . . they were my university! I continue the learning process now with my ground crew: Gabrielle; my other horse, Rollie; Alexandria, my cat; and Olivia, my dog.

The Legacy of Pet One and Pony Boy

With what I know now in terms of nutrition and behavior, I probably could have kept Pet One and Pony Boy alive. However, I've learned that even though they're no longer physically present, they're always in my heart. Animals have an intelligence and an understanding that's beyond our words, and I believe that there's a reason why they've incarnated as these beings, and we must respect the laws of their contract as that particular species.

Without going through that painful rite of passage, I wouldn't be able to help as many dogs, cats, horses, ferrets, turtles, zoo animals, and animals living in rehab . . . and all the people caring for them.

Here on Earth, we get to adapt with the circumstances, whether we call that change positive or negative, happy or sad. It's all an opportunity to move ourselves along. This work has been proof to me that we never know where an odyssey will take us, and that miracles exist in any given situation.

Obviously, part of Pet One and Pony Boy's covenant with me led me to write this book. It's work that we're collectively doing; my name will go on the cover simply because I'm still here in physical form (and I know how to type!). And the work is a continuum because you and I will be here together as you take in these words.

If I close my eyes, when I think of the familiarity of Pet One or the devotion of Pony Boy, it's as if no time has passed. And forward into the future, their impact will continue as the stories of other creatures that have benefited from this work will exponentially help even more people and animals. That's because many of the case studies contained herein will seem familiar to other individuals, mirroring *their* situation, and then they will make the adjustments to improve life in their own home.

All beings have their own karma or "stuff" they get to work through. When you connect with another—especially over something where the learning curve is so high, as mine was with Pet One and Pony Boy—it might be that you're reflecting something, that you get to really be of service to that being, or that the one you're linked to is the solid ground for *you* to grow from. Regardless, it's an opportunity for you to embody unconditional love, even when circumstances seem to go awry.

Some lessons are so big that you have to take notes and file them away. They could lead you to something you're unaware is even happening in the moment, which will have a great impact on future events. We humans are the ones who are tortured by reason. Animals work through their karma and don't question their existence. It's fabulous, really.

The power of the words around Pony Boy when he was deemed "evil" by others, or the original outpouring of sympathy for him when he was alone in the stall, created a formative environment. In quantum physics, the mind is shaping the very thing that is being perceived. Every day I see animals that seem to be trapped in a behavior or illness because of the perceptions around them. Sometimes all I do is come in and reframe the picture for the human so that the animal is freed from that bondage.

Not everyone has to go to the extreme of eating hay in a stall in order to get a "monkey see, monkey do" reaction out of another—but that was my journey to this work. Everyone is different. I guess I had to be conked over the head with it all because I, Joan, certainly wasn't getting that this was my path. I was seeing it as a tragedy that took over my life in the middle of my career in the film industry.

I can remember the two times I did go to psychics prior to these events. I was asking about some film I'd auditioned for. The psychics always said, "You're so intuitive—you're going to have to come to terms with that," and I'd think, *Yeah, yeah—whatever. Am I going to get the part?* You see, I was too dense to waltz into this as my life journey.

Your own rite of passage may be a decision or inkling that this is what you want to do—or perhaps, like me, your motivation might just be to have better communication.

Pony Boy was a perfect vibrational match for me, as my experience with him set me up to navigate through a maze of emotional madness several years later when I was the victim of a heinous crime. I seem to be compressing karma; and the big, tragic events lead me to a sense of deeper empathy. But being the victim of a crime was a real mind-bender. The perpetrator had a tragic setup very like Pony Boy's. After the initial shock, I was able to look with compassion upon that person.

In Native American cultures, when a hawk swoops down and grabs a rabbit, in the moment the rabbit's life ends it becomes one with the hawk. Ancient Egyptians believed in the Oneness. My Catholic upbringing taught me about redemption, and I've learned after all my experiences in life that every situation is an opportunity to recognize our connection or separation from that ever-present One Mind . . . a chance to readjust or realign. Our animal companions offer us that potential to connect with It daily through their patience, purity of spirit, and unconditional love.

About This Book

My intention in putting my years of experience and education into these pages is threefold. I want to:

1. Demystify "animal communication" and what it means to be a "pet psychic"

2. Have my many varied stories in this line of work act as a catalyst for deeper understanding in your own home, especially if you're facing a challenge with your beloved animals

3. Help you understand how much you're already tuning in to your nonhuman companions and offer simple techniques that will help you enhance that communication

In Part I, you'll see the different situations where I've come in to help as the animal communicator, the pet psychic, or the translator. The guidance that I've offered has been through seeing all the parts of the picture and coming up with a plan that creates something more supportive to the players involved. Ultimately, I'm just the interpreter: The humans who call me in for help are the real agents of change. Many of the ways that animal communication works are explained here, too.

In Part II, you'll find tools and simple guidelines to help you become a better communicator in your own home. It starts with awareness of, and then focus upon, the solution rather than the problem. By using some of the techniques for quieting your brain in order to receive information, you'll find that it's imperative to be a great *sender* of information. By being a leader in your household emotionally, you can allow your animal companions to respond in a more harmonious way—which will impact them, the humans in your family, and the world around you. (You'll also find some additional resources for better understanding and caring for your animals.)

PART I

Revelations of an Animal Communicator

❖ Chapter One ❖

DECODING ANIMAL COMMUNICATION

Ask the very beasts, and they will teach you;
ask the wild birds—they will tell you;
crawling creatures will instruct you,
fish in the sea will inform you:
for which of them all knows not that this is the Eternal's way,
in whose control lies every living soul,
and the whole life of man.
— Job 12:7–10

I wasn't born an animal communicator or a pet psychic (I didn't talk to ducks when I was a child). These are skills I learned, and I believe that we all can be animal communicators. As well as doing consulting work, I now teach basic communication and energy workshops so that pet guardians, breeders, trainers, and health-care practitioners can learn how to get the facts that lead to understanding their animals' problems and needs.

People flock to my classes to find out how to receive information from animals, thinking that this will make the communication between them better—but it's a two-way street (at the very least). In these pages, I hope you'll see not only how much you're already receiving, but also what you're presently sending. Learning to transmit better messages more effectively can enhance all aspects of your life.

3

What is considered "animal communication" is actually the use of telepathy: the sending or receiving of information by way of the subtle language of feelings, words, and pictures. Many of you have already experienced this phenomenon. Say that a loved one is away and you get a strong sensation about the person—a feeling or an urgency to connect with him or her. Later on that day you receive an e-mail, a phone call, or something in the mail from that very individual. We tend to dismiss such an event as a coincidence, but it's actually telepathy at work—and it's every bit as real as the bank statement that also came in the mail that day.

The world is made up of energy. We live in a dual reality:

1. There's that which we can see in tangible form before us, along with the energy around us that can come in via those feelings, words, and pictures.

2. Then there's the whole universal web of connections that already exists between all of us humans and with other life-forms.

You probably want to understand how this invisible communication and connection impacts your animals at home. Outside influences affect you—on any given day making you either joyful or depressed—and then your state of being becomes its own force of energy that can have a direct bearing on your animal companions. You'll begin to recognize through the stories you'll read that even a subtle shift within your own state of being will be felt by the nonhuman residents in your household or barn. Hopefully, as you make these subtle shifts and achieve more harmony with your animals at home, this will have a ripple effect on the rest of your universe.

Telepathy knows no time or space, so the majority of my work consists of sitting in my office doing a phone session while still wearing my riding clothes. The beauty of this is that I'm able to connect with many people and animals all over the country—and the globe, for that matter. Usually clients e-mail me pictures of their animals and then call me at the agreed-upon appointment time: I often have back-to-back bookings on phone days. I get very quiet and link up with the animals by way of the pictures, which hold their energy. I don't always work with photos, but they make life easier for me.

On the days when I don't have phone sessions, I do house calls. This involves going to someone's home and meeting the entire family—meaning both the humans and their animal companions. I also frequently go to a barn and in consecutive sessions meet a number of riders and their horses, helping all of them. My work is ever changing and never dull! On one day, it might be a dog that likes to sneak out of the yard and take himself for walks; on another, it could be a horse that wishes his owner had a better sense of humor! (You'll be reading more about these true cases later.)

The majority of people I deal with are having a behavioral or wellness challenge with their animal companions when they come to me for help. Usually by the time they call me, they've lost hope. After our session, I connect them with trainers, vets, or chiropractors, depending on what services they need. Sometimes I feel like the networking clearinghouse!

It's been a long road getting to where I am now . . . becoming that "go-to" person for individuals with challenging pets. As a child, I did feel very connected to animals, but I wasn't aware of hearing words or seeing pictures. Yet, as I look back, I believe that some images I subconsciously perceived held sway over my actions. I grew up in Washington State, and being in a forest at a young age—especially on a horse—I was not just conscious of, but also awakened to, the deep labyrinth of coexistence, which was exceptionally powerful and magical.

When we make a change, sometimes those closest to us have trouble accepting the shift. My newfound passion and life direction as an animal communicator was met with a healthy dose of skepticism and mocking remarks by my friends. A complete stranger with a cat that was shredding the furniture was more likely to embrace what I was doing!

One friend in particular made fun of me more than anyone else. Still, I offered to talk to her cat. My pal had broken up with a musician named John, and she was bereft. Many people had rallied in support of her in order to let her decompress her grief.

According to her, she hadn't seen John in months. When I communicated with the cat, I asked if she missed John. The cat let me know that she didn't because he was over there every night! That ended my friend's amusement at my expense, and she started laughing *with* me about some of the truly entertaining aspects of this work. That friend has now sent me many clients over the years. She also had a valuable experience, because she'd been "breaking up" with John as if she were trying on a dress for size, and after the truth was out, she had the strength to truly detach from him.

I don't necessarily recommend that anyone doing animal communication put themselves in the line of fire in that way, however. In this particular case, my friend and I knew each other very well and were conscious of what made the other tick, so the nature of our relationship wouldn't have changed whether I had picked up on anything from her cat or not. What I'm saying here is that there should be nothing to prove in doing this work.

When jumping into this world of animal communication—or making any big change, for that matter—feeling safe and having inner peace about the work is vital. Fortunately, my years working as an actress and writer in New York and Hollywood gave me a thick skin! While artists and healers share a deep sensitivity, the first group has to get up and keep going even if everyone says no. I've learned to roll with the punches.

Sometimes people call me for a consultation even when they don't really believe in animal communication. After doing it for ten years, I've developed a practical knowledge of both human and animal behavior, as well as grounding myself in nutrition and healing modalities, so I'm able to assist them in resolving their challenges in a myriad of ways. Most important, I continue learning, learning, and learning some more. For example, I study acupressure and read dog-training books all the time—I can't get enough.

Learning and practice are key to this work. There are some people who have more of a natural proclivity for intuition or telepathy than others, in the same way that Michael Jordan came out of the chute a better basketball player than I could ever be. I don't play the sport because I don't have the time, but I bet that if I learned the basics and practiced, I could play enough to have fun. With discipline, it will be easier for you to make progress in animal communication than it would be to try playing professional basketball!

Along with having an ability to cut out the chatter in your head and find a quiet place within, you need to have an open heart, develop compassion, learn to trust yourself, have a willingness to look through the lens of another, and then practice all of these life-enhancing tools. I believe that animal communication, telepathy, and energy work are all muscles that atrophy once we learn language. We *can* relearn them, though, once we're aware of what they are.

Telepathy Explained

Have you ever seen a flock of birds lift off from what seemed to be a peacefully grounded moment? Suddenly, they take flight as if they were all tuned in to the same radio frequency. One bird hones in on unrest and transmits a sense of fear or urgency to the group in a matter of seconds . . . and away they go. The same goes for a herd of horses, a pack of dogs, and many other members of the animal kingdom.

Animals communicate telepathically with each other—when they're tuned in. Of course, they were all also given "voices," which can be used as signals to one another or to us. If you have an animal companion, you most likely know the difference between your dog's bark, cat's meow, horse's neigh, or bird's coo when your pet

is saying, "Hey, hey, hey—hi, hi, hi!" "Look at me," or
even "Oh my God, I can't believe you don't see this!" Of
course, there are a million other greetings or demands. A
Jack Russell terrier may feel really small down there and
need a guarantee of acknowledgment, whereas a border
collie might bark to move someone through a crowd.

Sometimes, though, our understanding of what our
animal companions are trying to tell us gets lost in translation, and our two-way communication with them goes
awry. It may be an illness or a behavior that has us baffled
. . . or a horse that's supposed to be a soul mate is bucking
. . . or we have a cat, the sentry, the overseer of all, yet
he still urinates on the couch . . . or a beloved family dog
has been nipping the neighbor's kid. Or perhaps we have
such a profound, intense relationship with our animal
companion that we want to know more. How many of us
would love to discover that there's deeper thought going
on than just: *Throw me the ball?*

I certainly don't mean to diminish the value of
"Throw me the ball." *Au contraire.* Decompressing your
day with a lively session of fetch may be just what the
universe ordered. And when else do we grown-ups allow
ourselves the time or the space to enjoy something like
that? In our world, play doesn't appear to be productive.
However, who better than your animal companion to
share the opportunity for a smile and a laugh—a moment
of precision, of joy, of . . . well, I could go on and on.
Perhaps it's just a chance to share, with no identification,
qualification, or quantification. Only adult human minds
need to define these moments. Kids and animals have
cornered the market on lighthearted, free feelings. Why
not enjoy them, too?

By the time somebody connects with me for a consultation, they may very well want to do so for pleasure,

fun, or entertainment, but more likely it's the result of a behavioral or physical situation. I might add that I'm usually at the end of the line, the last call for help. Some of the problems are herd/pack related; some are people difficulties. For the most part, it's fair to assume that the issue will be a people *perception* problem. When you unpack this concept, you can say one of two things:

1. I'm looking at this situation strictly from my viewpoint—my belief system—and actually projecting all of my experience onto what *appears* to be a problem.

2. I'm focusing on a seeming problem; therefore, nothing will change except that perhaps now I have a bigger one!

So to get beyond those hurdles, why *not* employ telepathy? This is the forgotten original communication . . . as a baby, you were dependent on it. In the beginning, sounds, screaming, and crying were simply a way of getting attention or making a plea for help. Eventually you learned words, and as your language developed, your telepathic muscle lost tone.

But still, telepathy is going on all the time even if you aren't fully aware of it—whether you like it or not. It's evident when you tend to speak in code with your friends. This goes beyond intimacy . . . it's the passing of images back and forth. Doubtless, you've often known which friend or family member was on the other end of the ringing phone, even in the days before this information was confirmed by caller ID. So many of us have had an experience like that with a loved one.

And you don't even need an intimate connection. You experience telepathy when you've been able to finish a complete stranger's sentence. Then there are the times that through a rough form of pantomime, you can figure out what a foreigner is asking and are even able to give the person directions. Although aided by the physical gestures, by intuiting what they need, or by just having the good luck of being able to figure things out, again, a series of pictures has been passed back and forth between you.

As I mentioned, telepathy knows no time or space. When you're having persistent thoughts and can't get someone who lives far away out of your head and then a letter from that individual appears in the mail, that's no coincidence—that's you being tuned in. There's no beginning and no end to it; it just *is*. This is happening all the time, with information and images being sent and received like ocean waves.

Telepathy can be active or nonactive, so it's not as if you have to sit and "do" it. Your state of being can be broadcasting something whether you're aware of it or not, which is why when you're in physical pain or are sick, your dog or cat will frequently want to take care of you. If you're emotionally hurt or are fearful about the security of your job, that day your horse may be even more protective of you while going over a jump. If you're distracted or can't concentrate because you're overwhelmed by your thoughts, one of your animal companions might be more entertaining in order to get you out of your own head.

Our state of being attracts or repels people and animals around us. It's our frequency or vibration transmitted by our emotions, thoughts, or physical condition.

This could be as basic as the fact that we smell funny from taking a medication or that we're depressed from popping a painkiller. Either way, the larger world around us and our own microcosm (that is, our homes) responds, just as *we* are constantly responding to the stimulation, frequency, or vibration of what we're exposed to—say, a spouse, a boss, a friend in a tough situation, a traffic jam, Fox News. . . .

Introducing One Mind

I've talked about the concept that we're sending and receiving thoughts and images without any effort. Take that one step further and imagine yourself as a holographic being, and picture your soul taking form. See it as connected to whatever your belief is: God, the Universe, the Great Spirit, the Holy Spirit, Allah, Buddha, the Divine, the Force, the Oneness, spirit guides, your Higher Self, or all the angels and saints. Out of respect for however you perceive it, I'll call it "One Mind" for our purposes.

Now, for a moment, feel the weightlessness of One Mind. It holds a frequency, a vibration, which is lighter than a thought such as: *Oh, I forgot to pick up my clothes at the dry cleaner's.* That simple phrase could bring up mayhem, because who knows what else has slipped your mind? You could remember all of those other things just when you're trying to concentrate on *nothing.* Then add a little spit on the ball by thinking about an event or a serious issue that you have going on in your life, and suddenly the density of that worry holds yet more weight. It may even stimulate a physiological response such as a nervous tummy or a fluttering of your heart. These thoughts and feelings whirl around like a flock of birds suddenly scattering, and eventually they create an energetic pattern.

Getting back to the animals, you can imagine what they're thinking when you walk through the door in this state: *Uh-oh, we better entertain her.* They feel helpless because they've habitually tried to lift your spirits or distract you, and this time it isn't effective; the spam thoughts have taken hold of the whole household. After a while, they could get sullen or resort to bad behavior. This is animal communication just as surely as what I do, since you're inadvertently sending out dense thoughts and uncomfortable feelings.

People often say to me, "Animals are so spiritual." I don't know that they're any more or less so than we are. They're definitely clued in to One Mind in a way that we're not. Because of this, they sense something without knowing it, and they just operate from instinct—for example, the "fight or flight" principle. They can perceive danger from One Mind . . . they are just *being.*

Years ago I moved to Denver after living in Los Angeles. When it snowed, I was *really* cold. I often let that bother me, in addition to the marital problems that weighed heavily on me. I'll never forget walking my dog, Olivia, one night after a big snowfall. We went down the hill and she sniffed along, curious to see who else had been out in the fresh snow. When it came time for us to turn around, we had to go back up the big hill. Well, I groaned just thinking about it. She, on the other hand, trotted up the slope as if to say, "It's a hill. Big deal, *I get* to run up it." But really she didn't even give it a thought; there was no motivation behind it or acknowledgment of it: It just was. Even with all that I'd been doing in this line of work and on my path of spiritual growth, I had to see her trotting up the hill, simply because she could, in order to "get" the simplicity of One Mind.

Animals' ability to just *be* and not question their existence makes them seem more spiritual. We humans are so far away from "just being" in our everyday life. If it isn't bills, it's taxes; if it isn't taxes, it's what color to paint the bathroom; if it isn't the bathroom, it's forgetting to send off an RSVP for that party . . . it's always something. As a result, there are miscommunications and breakdowns in our behavior. Or we have unclear ideas about how to proceed when our pets get sick. Ultimately, the depth of love that animals express to us is so profound that there are no words to explain it.

Sometimes the greatest thing you can do—even if you don't necessarily believe that it's communication *per se* or that you'll get any secret messages from your animals—is to just "be" with them and connect on that level of One Mind. It doesn't require any activity: You don't have to pet them in that moment; you don't have to brush them right then . . . you don't have to do anything. Just be in their space. Sometimes that's all they're waiting for.

Animals don't perceive themselves as separate. Yes, a feeling can arise for them in a given situation. It can be momentary or last as long as we want to hold them to it. Our perception of their emotions, added to our own about the situation, creates a box for them that inhibits their innate behavior. In the terms of quantum physics, the very thing we perceive is being shaped as we perceive it. According to the theory of *quantum interconnectedness*, if two objects are joined and then pulled apart, what remains is a "stickiness" between them, thus keeping them linked.

For instance, when one animal crosses over, the others naturally grieve, as do we. Every fiber of the household contains that emotion. Even human-made things started out as organic materials, and they hold energy. Thus, a home could become haunted by your feelings, and ultimately, the occupants could almost suffocate in that atmosphere.

For many people, animals represent an object of unconditional love, and I also believe that most of the time that's what they're showing us. But for some folks, that's still *"conditional* unconditional" love—as in, it's unconditional until they put their hand in their bird's cage and it bites them.

Whether you believe in past and future lives or feel that we only have this one, there's still a collective consciousness from the beginning of life on this planet that we can tap into. One Mind includes this, as well as the following:

- Universal intelligence through lifetimes
- The cause and effect of karma
- All-encompassing unconditional love
- That purity of Spirit we see when we look into our animal companions' eyes

It's like being on an observation deck, where we can get as close as we possibly can to a neutral perspective that still comes from a place of love.

THE MYTH OF MULTITASKING

One of the biggest detours from One Mind is the misperception that we can multitask. Our brains weren't set up for it, yet we all insist that we can do it. For example, I continue to sweep up dog and cat hair while chatting on the phone with friends. I do try to limit myself as to how far I'll go with multitasking, because scientific experiments support the notion that it tends to backfire.

My dog, Olivia, and I conducted our own multitasking experiments. This is something that you can try at home. All you need is a dog (or any other species) that's relatively interested in retrieving and two objects to be fetched.

Just so you have a clear picture of our experiments, Olivia's mother is a border collie, and her father was half German shepherd and half rottweiler. All three breeds are smarty-pants . . . and needless to say, Olivia is frequently too clever for her own good. When it comes to playing with objects, she sinks right into the border-collie half and is downright obsessive. If another dog is around, she can be very competitive and even sneaky. Just to crystallize this picture for you, there are balls—and other toys—all over my house: In fact, Olivia considers the furniture to be a safe-deposit box. At some point during the day, she'll look under a piece of furniture, and lo and behold, there's yet another ball that she has saved.

So the experiment goes like this: Her eyes bear down on the ball in my hand. When I throw it, she catches it in the air like a champ. Then, when she's gloating a bit over how great that was with plans to hang on to it, I immediately toss her another ball. You don't have to be a pet psychic to picture the thought process: *Do I catch the ball? But I have to drop this one. Is there a way to catch the other ball with this one in my mouth? Hmm, I'll have to put the first ball down, I think. I might be able to catch the other one.*

At this point, the ball is milliseconds from her nose. She jumps to catch it, and guess what? She loses both balls. Sometimes she'll drop one and catch the other. The reality is, she can't catch the new one *and* hold on to the old one. By trying to do two things at once, there's simply confusion, verging on chaos. She wants both so badly that she can hardly concentrate on maintaining one or seizing the other.

We humans aren't any farther down the road as far as perfecting multitasking. We can delegate activities to others, and we can

---

THE MYTH OF MULTITASKING, CONT'D.

prioritize—that's about it. We can *try* to do a couple of things at once, but usually neither gets done or they both turn out badly. And our minds are certainly not quiet at that point and definitely not receptive.

Sadly, this is the state of most of us in this frenzied, overstimulated world. We're missing the best opportunities to just have a fun moment with our animal companions because we're trying to do everything at once. We aren't *being* anything, but we're *doing* a lot. (If we *are* being anything, it's chaotic!)

A Matter of Interpretation

My job as an animal communicator is to go in and listen to what the animals have to say and give them messages from the humans. From there, I then relay to people how their messages are being interpreted by the animals, and I'm able to start to reframe the picture for their guardians. While I can tell a cat to use the litter box, it's going to be more important for his human to change how *she* is sending that message. If the person is still envisioning yet another piece of furniture being destroyed by cat urine, then it doesn't matter how psychic I am. The cat will think, *Oh yeah, this pet-psychic yahoo lady came over and told me not to pee on the fancy couch. Well, my person expects it, so watch this!*

One-third of my job is the communication with the animal: That's the pet-psychic bit. The second part is communication with the human—being the messenger to and from the animal. The last third is forming a plan with the person to make household adjustments to support the pet's new behavior, performance, or wellness.

We're the managing partners, and most of the time people have to buck up on their oversight skills. We also have to make up a new natural order for all the players. It's the humans who have to be willing to assume leadership in their thoughts and feelings. *This* is as much animal communication as the pet-psychic bit.

Compassion and understanding for all parties is also a very important component. People are where they are, when they're there. If clients have gone to the trouble of contacting me—even if they're resistant to what I'm saying at the time—somewhere deep in their being, they wanted a change or they wouldn't have called me.

If I don't communicate well to the human involved, there's no chance of setting up a change for the animal. I always tell students in my classes that if they don't like people, then this isn't the job for them. As a profession, animal communication requires respect and compassion for all, even when what a client does isn't what I would do. When people don't know something, it's my job to enlighten them gently, encouraging them to try another way. If I put them off, they'll get defensive, which doesn't help their pet. Worse, they'll rebel against what I've said, and that *really* doesn't serve the animal. Sure, I can be passionate about an issue, but even then, I have to accept that I have no control over the outcome.

There are very few people in the scheme of things who have purely bad intentions; mostly they're just misguided. There are even fewer animals with negative motives—and of that small percentage, it's usually due to circumstances or some genetic nightmare. And most often what can appear to be bad or wrong is truly a perception and then a communication breakdown . . . and that very nearly always starts with humans.

❖ *Chapter Two* ❖

BECOMING AWARE

If all the beasts were gone, man would die from a great loneliness
of spirit. For whatever happens to the beasts, soon happens to man.
All things are connected. . . . Whatever befalls the earth befalls the
sons of the earth.
— Chief Seattle of the Suquamish tribe,
in a letter to President Franklin Pierce

Sometimes one of the biggest obstructions to understanding what our animals are experiencing and
needing is being in an all-consuming state as a result of
a painful experience. By being so far from One Mind, we
get confused about how to care for our animals' needs
when they start acting up.

Perception Breakdown

In the world of theater, there's an old saying pertain-
ing to performing: "*Mood* spelled backward is *doom.*" This
can be true in our own households. When we have an
epic, life-changing situation or are facing the loss of our
pet, everyone under our roof gets consumed by the pall

that's cast over every apsect of our lives. Awareness is the first step to freeing the household from this dynamic.

Annie and Bob

Annie came to me wanting to know why her cat, Bob, seemed very depressed. She suspected that it might be a territorial issue with the cat next door. I got quiet and connected with Bob. According to him, Annie had experienced a life-altering falling-out with what appeared to be her father or a father figure. Bob felt that Annie was resigned and grieving, having lost her inner fight. He was resolute that this was the issue and really couldn't have cared less if the cat next door jumped onto their terrace and taunted him through the window.

When I described what Bob had relayed to me, Annie was astonished by how much awareness he had about her life. She told me that while she was in college, she'd been the victim of sexual harassment by one of her professors. Without articulating it, she indicated that it went further than harassment—it was molestation. The professor was lauded as a paternal figure and actually had been a stronger presence in her life than her own father. Annie had found out that she wasn't the only one this had happened to and was deciding whether or not to join with the other women in the lawsuit that had been filed. Bob wanted her to get her inner fight back, for herself and his home life, whether she pressed charges or not.

Many clients ask at this point if the communication comes to me in the form of a conversation with the animal—and sometimes it does. More important, though, is picking up on concepts. Animals send how they send, and I perceive how I perceive. Every connection is different, but some of Annie and Bob's story came in the form of images, the strongest one being of Annie bereft. When I showed Bob a picture of the looming cat next door, it held no emotional charge for him, so I knew that he wasn't bothered by the neighboring cat, but he *was* nearly overwhelmed by Annie's emotional state and couldn't penetrate it. He couldn't comfort or entertain her; he felt useless. The concept of the father figure was more like an impression, one that at first I was convinced was her real father. *Inner fight* came in words, and the feeling of loss was completely pervasive.

Customarily in a session—unless it's a direct question-and-answer period near the end—I tend to write down the images, words, and impressions. Then I sit with the animal for a moment before I begin saying what I picked up on. While I can perceive this information and conceptualize it, the form I received it in may not be the same as the one it was sent in.

Frank and Christian

Sometimes animals are caught in a painful state because of the mixed messages that are being sent back and forth between their human guardians. For example, if an animal is sick, we may not know what the right thing to do is because our own emotions about the situation get in the way. Or we feel guilty because we could have prevented it or because the choices we're making have an immediate effect. We forget, of course, that the animals have their own journey. And maybe by being in One Mind with them, we can just enjoy whatever time is left.

Years ago my friend Frank called me, saddened by the idea that he should put down his beloved dog that day. Christian was a 12-year-old golden retriever who had been Frank's companion for years through many ups and downs in his life. At this point, Christian could barely walk. Frank had to help him up and felt guilty about spending more active time with Devlin, his seven-year-old golden.

I connected telepathically with Christian and was surprised by what I found out. I had a sense that his lungs and heart were a bit taxed, but Christian told me he wasn't ready to "go" right now: He wanted to have a party.

"A party?" Frank asked in disbelief.

"A party," I repeated emphatically.

That day, Frank took Christian to the vet, who let him know that the golden retriever had bronchitis. The dog was given some antibiotics and sent home. Frank then planned the festivities.

When the day came, Christian sat in a corner basking in the sun. Kids jumped on the trampoline, while the adults were either aghast or amused that they'd all gathered for the fabricated birthday of a dog. Frank brought out the cake and gathered everyone to sing "Happy Birthday." As the song began, Christian shot up, *ran* over to Frank, and sat there, howling through the words. Nobody could believe it. No more than a week later, Christian had a heart attack and died in the hallway—it was very fast, and he was at home. *And* he'd gotten to have his party.

Thankfully, Frank had realized that he wasn't clear enough to know what to do as Christian's condition was declining before his very eyes, and he'd called for a session. The dog got to have a say in what happened to him, and his people entertained his wishes. In the end, it was a beautiful closing to a very important chapter of Frank's life.

James and Belle

James called me to schedule a visit to his farm because his horse was bucking him off. When I went out there, I could sense from both James and the beautiful mare, Belle, that the relationship had been that of animal/human soul mates.

James and Belle were both devastated by the situation. James was hurt and angry, and he felt as if he were failing. He'd never been so close with a being, yet the horse was tossing him up in the air like a lightweight stuffed animal, and he was at an age when bones don't mend quickly. The worst part of it for James was that he felt betrayed by the love of his life, this magnificent mare.

When I connected with Belle, the image of an impasse or a standoff kept coming up. She felt that James wasn't getting the fact that her back was very sore and that the minute she saw the saddle, she knew it was going to make her suffer physically. Her feelings were hurt, as James had been so attentive up until this point, and it was disturbing to her that he was ignoring this most basic need.

By being stuck in his own feelings about the situation, James couldn't see his horse's true, simple wishes. Even when I told him of her pain, he remained locked into the betrayal . . . until I poked Belle's back right where she said that the discomfort was and her legs buckled. He finally saw with his own eyes that the horse wasn't in any way, shape, or form betraying him; rather, she was just communicating that she needed help. If he wasn't going to hear her subtle message—for instance, when she moved away as the saddle was going on—she would have to resort to more dramatic methods of communication.

James immediately sought out an equine chiropractor, and once Belle was adjusted, they were back to being in love again. A couple of years later, James called and thanked me profusely because they were doing so great that sometimes they were going on the trail twice a day! And he was staying on top of her bodywork.

Loyalty

Animals are always loyal in communication sessions. Even if there's a perception breakdown and the household has run amok, they still make their feelings known from a place of love. Sometimes people are afraid that their dog or cat is going to "tell" on them. This still cracks me up even after years of doing this work, because this is anything but the case. The only information that gets exposed is exactly what needs to come out in order to improve the situation.

On occasion, animals will reveal some quirky behavior of their "person." For example, a 20-something gal came over to have a reading of her two adorable little dachshunds. One of them told me that his person sang a lot in the middle of the night. The young woman confirmed that when she couldn't sleep, she got out of bed and did karaoke! I don't think any loyalty was breached there, and we had a great laugh.

Beth and Petunia

Sometimes animals send me a concept wrapped in symbolism to protect their person, yet it still relays a message. A woman named Beth had me over to talk to her three cats, one of which had been sick, and Beth wanted to know if it was her time. That day—that minute—it wasn't.

The main concern of the cat, Petunia, was how grateful she was that after two years, Beth had come out from under what looked like a giant sticky web and was now going back to work. Petunia had been very helpful to Beth while she was under this "web."

Well, Beth was astonished. She revealed to me that the web was breast cancer, and she'd been very sick. After battling the disease, she'd finally won and was indeed reentering the working world.

This came as an image, an impression of her being nearly suffocated by this thing—the "cancer web." Knowing what a struggle this was for her, given the public's perception of sickness, Petunia was very protective of Beth and loyal to her. It's not our animals' job to "out us" about our feelings or circumstances. Without being specific about a painful experience or blowing open our deepest, darkest secret, they will relay enough information to let me know how much their human's lifestyle, work habits, or interpersonal relationships have impacted them.

COMMUNICATION WITH ALL LIFE

Mary and Ringo

Mary called me as a result of having problems with her dog. I walked into her lovely townhouse, which had artwork on the floor waiting to be hung. The dog, Ringo, was a small, white, very cute guy who was tremendously excited to see me. Mary warned me as I entered that he had aggression issues with visitors. Thankfully, he refrained from displaying this behavior (although it wouldn't have been the first dog bite I'd suffered while doing this work).

A dog trainer had waited with Mary for my arrival. I sat down and asked Mary the usual questions:

- What's your dog's name?
- How old is he?
- How long have you had him?
- Are you two the only ones in the household?

And from there, I got quiet and asked Ringo what was going on. The dog told me that *everything* seemed out of control. He informed me that Mary had been a victim of a heinous crime and that she'd been forced to move immediately and assume another identity. Plus, she had sustained other losses (it felt like a death and a breakup). Ringo also let me know that there had been something wrong with him when he was born, and even though the breeder didn't sell him to be a show dog, he'd turned out handsome after all. He told me that he was in trouble a lot and let me in on a few other small details. Then with a giant sigh, he went to sleep.

Mary commented, "Wow, I've never seen him so quiet with new people here."

I told her that Ringo had gotten a big story off of his chest, and that now he could relax. For some animals, being able to tell their personal history is enough to shift the energy.

I proceeded to relate to Mary exactly what Ringo had told me. Upon hearing the first part about the crime, the woman just stared at me in disbelief and couldn't lift her jaw back up. At that point, the dog trainer was uncomfortable and asked if he should leave the room. Obviously, with the move Mary was starting over, and nobody in her new life needed to know what she'd run from.

We both said no. I assured Mary that her dog was loyal to her and didn't tell me the specifics of the incident. He only mentioned it because it had such a profound effect on both of their lives that he couldn't hold back anymore. I also let her know that the crime was none of my business, and she didn't need to tell me details unless she felt that it was necessary.

"You know, I didn't even believe in this—I was just doing it because the dog trainer was at a loss," she said.

When I finished with the dog's story, Mary confirmed for me that there had indeed been a breakup; in fact, her ex-boyfriend was the perpetrator of the crime. As it turns out, Mary shared the details of how he'd tried to kill her. The old boyfriend had obviously been someone Ringo also loved and trusted. As a result, the dog didn't reveal who the perpetrator had been. While the crime was being committed, Ringo hid under the bed.

The dog was struggling with his own fear, frustration, sadness, and incompetence, as well as post-traumatic stress disorder (PTSD) over the event. Simultaneously, he was picking up on Mary's fear, betrayal, depression, loss, desperation, and of course, her own PTSD.

Also, Mary's mother had died around the same time she got Ringo—the other big loss that she was dealing with. And Mary confirmed that he had some sort of lining around his eye that wouldn't be acceptable in a show ring, but it cleared up within the first year. While the love between Mary and Ringo was evident, she admitted to being very frustrated and irritated with him.

To make matters worse, the dog *knew* that he was constantly disappointing Mary no matter what he tried to do, so it was a vicious circle. Ringo obviously needed to feel mini-triumphs in everyday life rather than always being in trouble.

This is the heart of communication with animals. As much as we'd like to think that it's about getting quiet on a mountaintop and hearing their voices or seeing them as some greater spiritual being, it's really rather pedestrian.

Actions communicate plenty. Being able to objectively look at the behavior and disconnect your feelings from it is a great place to start. Learning to still your mind in the face of the hectic world we're living in helps. In this case, what Ringo was clearly communicating through his behavior was: "Hey, I'm scared and don't know how to act, so to protect you, I'll bite whoever comes in the house. But I'm still terrified that strangers could do something bad, so I'll pee at the door, too, because I can't contain it." At the same time, Mary was entrenched in her circumstances; she was navigating through her own unpleasant emotions, *and* she was completely exasperated by the behavior of the dog and couldn't see past the idea that he was purposely frustrating her.

Once the communication happened, Mary softened her feelings about Ringo's behavior. Granted, she still had her own PTSD to work through. Nevertheless, at that point, she did have more compassion for Ringo because she'd been enlightened about the fact that he, too, was going through this with her. Being vigilant about self-awareness equates to being compassionate.

Compassion and awareness of her feelings *that minute* and how they affected the dog still might not have been enough in a situation like that. Believe it or not, the biggest healing component possible right then was continued training for Ringo. Because both Beth and her dog were suffering as a result of the same event and had so many similar feelings, training would not only be useful, but also a great self-esteem-building distraction, in this case for both pet and guardian. They needed a win-win in their relationship.

Until then, even the dog trainer had been ready to give up and felt defeated by what he perceived to be the circumstances. Having this in-depth information also gave *him* a new starting point.

Evolution

It could be argued that the players in these stories are anthropomorphizing—that is, ascribing human characteristics to their pets. Maybe. Maybe not. All members of our household have a right to their feelings and their history; we can't take that away. But we *can* shift the perspective, which could create a shakedown that leads everyone to eventually coexist—or even better, to live together with joy.

These days, you'd be hard-pressed to find anyone who believes that animals don't have feelings. (Of course,

some people don't care, or animals aren't their "thing.")
But the naysayers have a tough argument, and the cards
are very much stacked against them. Furthermore, the
intelligence of animals is frequently measured in the
terms of *our* world. And there alone, they're evolving
right along with us, even though their brains may not
have the capacity that ours do. (In some circumstances I
think, *Lucky them!*) Or we're evolving *because* of them. In
fact, without horses in particular, we humans wouldn't be
where we are today—they've helped us build civilization.
That same goes for oxen, donkeys, and elephants.

Dr. Temple Grandin is a designer of livestock-
handling facilities and a professor of animal science at
Colorado State University. She's also perhaps the most
accomplished and well-known adult with autism in the
world. In her book *Animals in Translation,* she states:

> When you compare human and animal brains,
> the only difference that's obvious to the naked eye is
> the increased size of the *neocortex* in people. . . . The
> neocortex is the top layer of the brain, and includes the
> frontal lobes as well as all of the other structures where
> higher cognitive functions are located.

Grandin explains that the human neocortex is thick
and is the size of a peach pit, while that of animals is
much smaller. The bigger the neocortex, the more intelligence we can expect from a species. She also goes on to
say that we all share the same three brain regions and,
therefore, have three different intelligences or places to
process: (1) the reptilian brain; (2) the middle—paleomammalian—brain; and (3) the neomammalian brain,
which is the latest to develop and the highest in our
heads. She states:

... the reptilian brain corresponds to that in lizards and performs basic life support functions like breathing; the paleomammalian brain corresponds to that in mammals and handles emotion; and the neomammalian brain corresponds to that in primates—especially people—and handles reason and language. All animals have some neomammalian brain, but it's much larger and more important in primates and in people.

In the 1980s and '90s, Dr. Giacomo Rizzolatti at the University of Parma, Italy, discovered that monkeys may have a neuron that's responsible for "monkey see, monkey do" activities. However, it became clearer and clearer to him that this neuron truly was triggered by intentionality.

The studies followed the mirror neuron in relation to how we learn language; and this same nerve cell has been found in macaque monkeys, humans, and birds. Since then, scientists have discovered that people with autism may not have it or it might not be firing in those individuals.

So, what does it mean when it *is* fully firing? It signifies that we have the ability to feel, hear, see, taste, and understand what another is going through. We can perceive the intention behind someone's behavior rather than simply mimicking it. There's a special place in our brain that responds—and perhaps causes us to jump—when someone is shot in a movie, or that gets thrilled by and identifies with what an athlete is doing in a great competition. Our reaction is based on our engagement with that other world that we're watching. When we're lost in a state of our own, we have no way of deciphering this sort of information. So the next time your partner gets riled up over a football game, remind him of how in tune his mirror neuron is so that when the game is over, he can go into the kitchen and talk to the dog!

As Temple Grandin stated, our brains are more developed than those of animals, but many of the same components are shared by different species. I don't want to dwell on the science of telepathy; I'm more interested in the art of allowing this information to come through. However, it's nice to know that there are studies proving what intuitive folks and trainers were already aware of.

We do have the ability to understand the feelings and thoughts of our animals. Taken a step further, we can interpret their actions if we're able to get quiet enough to examine what their intention is through their feelings and thoughts. Awareness of this—and more important, of what's driving the behavior—will have an impact on our nonhuman housemates.

Animals that have been domesticated and are living in our homes are, of course, still after the basics in life such as food, water, and safety, but their awareness of our world is heightened. They're sifting through it—through *our* thoughts and *our* pictures—in order to get a sense of their own security. They're trying to penetrate this madness with their own thinking, and then they resort to communicating with us through behavior. Some of it is, by our standards, acceptable; some is true to their species and breeding; and some is just plain negative for our home environment. The not-so-good conduct is a result of our sending mixed messages or some human in their past having done so.

As much as we want to become aware of *their* thoughts and feelings, the first key is becoming aware of our own. Otherwise, we're looking through the lens of our own perceptions. The more we can take a step back and get to the observation deck of the One Mind, the more deeply connected we can become. And then animal communication is just ongoing.

Marianne and Sparky

Years ago when I lived in Los Angeles, a client by the name of Marianne used to call and set up an appointment a week ahead of time, only to cancel on the scheduled day. She said that her husband, Larry, didn't believe in animal communication. He was a screenwriter who worked from home, and she always arranged for sessions when she thought he would be at a studio meeting. After several times, I swore to myself that I wasn't even going to answer Marianne's calls, as this was very frustrating. Then one day I picked up, and she said her dog was going to be put down. Could I please come to the animal hospital?

When I got there, Marianne was in the back room. Sparky, her Labrador retriever, was very old and had struggled with Rocky Mountain spotted fever. Marianne was overwhelmed by the variety of problems that the disease had caused and by the secondary illnesses and other issues that she'd been handling as the dog aged. She was beside herself and wanted to know if Sparky was ready to go.

Sparky told me that she *was* ready, but not today. She wanted to go home and say good-bye to Marianne's husband, the home, and the other dog—an animal that she didn't necessarily love or even like, but which had been her companion. She needed one last night with the family. Marianne wasn't thrilled. This was a devastating situation, and it's so difficult to be ready to let go of a loved one. Not only did she not want to acknowledge the dog's feelings (even though she'd called me to learn what they were), she couldn't handle another agonizing day of watching Sparky struggle. Marianne seemed quite annoyed with me and with what I'd told her.

The vet then popped his head in and asked what the dog wanted! I said, "Sparky wants to go home to say good-bye and do this tomorrow."

The vet replied, "That's what *I* said." Then he left as quickly as he appeared—the sound of the door shutting was like an exclamation point. I'd done my job and now I had to leave. The outcome was out of my hands.

But it turned out beautifully. Even though Marianne had geared up for this event all day and had intended— and was prepared—to let go of Sparky, she listened to what her dog wanted and took her home. Marianne even told her husband, Larry, the nonbeliever, about the session.

Sparky hadn't really walked well in a very long time. Larry pulled out an old wagon and put her in it. Then he, Marianne, Sparky, and Hannah (the other dog) went on a hike over all the old fire roads that they'd walked for years. When they got home, Marianne and Larry made a big dinner and sat with the two dogs and reviewed Sparky's life. Sparky crossed over the next day. That simple communication led to a great send-off, one fully honoring her spirit.

❖ Chapter Three ❖

FEELINGS, WORDS, AND PICTURES

Dogs are wise. They crawl away into a quiet corner and lick their
wounds and do not rejoin the world until they are whole once more.
— Agatha Christie

I've already described how telepathy is the transference
of feelings, words, and pictures. But what exactly does
this mean?

Our minds work through pictures. Even if we don't
mean to, our thoughts are always creating visuals that
we're sending out. Every time we say a word, deep in our
brain we associate an image with it. Think of how many
camera shutters are clicking when the paparazzi follow a
star getting out of a limousine at a red-carpet event. That
is exactly what's happening in our brains.

We have our own thoughts and feelings, but we may
or may not be aware of how many additional ones we're
flooded with coming from friends, family, people we work
closely with, or even world events. All the while those ideas
and emotions are coming and going, associated images are

filtering through our system on an ongoing basis. Even if we say to our dog, "Don't bark," the snapshot we actually send is that of barking.

Feelings, words, and pictures work in concert. I'm going to break them down here, starting with feelings, because after years and years of teaching animal communication, I've found that they're the easiest to pick up on.

Feelings and Emotions

Feelings are like ocean waves: They wash up and they wash away. For animals, though, they move lightning fast. Your pets can be bored to tears or asleep, hear the clink of your keys, and become as excited as though it were Christmas morning and Santa just delivered a sack full of toys. Their feelings can go from 0 to 60 in a second—and back down again: "Oh, you have to return phone calls? I'll just be on the couch." They don't judge.

However, we *do* judge ourselves for negative feelings, and this becomes a pattern we grow accustomed to. Even if we don't like it, it becomes akin to old comfortable shoes that we don't want to throw out because we'll have to break in a new pair.

We also pass around low-grade emotions like a virus—the "feeling flu" is transmitted back and forth between beings in households or workplaces. Many of those I pick up on from animals originate with their person. When feelings are turned inward and aren't addressed, they can create illness.

Animals' emotions open the door to understanding their whole personality, as well as exposing how they function in the world. Are they pleaser types? Are they leaders? Are they always afraid that the other shoe is going to drop? Do they prefer to be one in a crowd? Are they driven more by what people want or by the leader of the pack, herd, or flock? Are these their autonomous feelings, or are they hooked onto those of humans? Examining how animals feel helps one figure out what would be the best adjustment to make to improve their lives.

The worst offender in terms of driving many mishaps in human/animal relationships is, of course, fear—it's like an infectious disease. A healthy respect is one thing, but fear is quite another. Many people become afraid of their birds after one bite. Others are scared to play with their cat because it gets overstimulated after a certain point and swats at them. Still others become afraid of their horses after hitting the ground once or twice. Some people fear what their dog will do after having a single bad experience. Animals feel this and quickly respond.

Jane and Remington

One afternoon I was out at a barn talking to the horses. The riders at this particular stable were predominantly teenagers who did three-day eventing. This is a riding discipline based, as you might imagine, on three different events: The first day is dressage, the second is cross-country jumping, and the third is stadium jumping. It's a tough and exciting sport, and you have to be pretty flexible and relatively competitive to participate. In order to qualify for the Olympics, you really have to be a bit of an adrenalin junkie.

Jane, a 13-year-old flanked by her parents, clutched a pad and pen, anxiously waiting to hear what her horse,

Remington, had to say. Immediately, he told me that he wanted her to know that she was a good enough rider. He was aware that Jane was plagued by the idea that he'd done very well with the previous girl who had ridden him, and Jane felt that she couldn't compare. Remington really wanted her to know that his relationship with her was much deeper, they were a better team, and she was just as good as the other girl, if not better. He gave me details as to the how and why of this.

When I told Jane, she burst into tears in front of all her peers, because this insecurity about not being good enough was her secret fear. Her relief was palpable, and there wasn't a dry eye in the barn aisle. Everyone else knew what a great team they were, and her parents were comforted, but Jane still carried this fear that needed addressing.

Jane asked why Remington stopped at the water jump. I asked him and then relayed the message to her: He felt that as they came down the hill toward the jump, she started mentally freezing up. He sensed her fear and stopped about four feet short.

"He thinks you're afraid," I said. Jane thought about that for a moment. The looks on her parents' faces confirmed for me that she had some timidness around that jump. I told her that she couldn't be scared, because that feeling ultimately caused her to physically tense ever so slightly, and that was like putting the brakes on for the horse. She had to visualize them leaping over the water repeatedly and then, when she was confident in that picture, take Remington to a course and start practicing until that jump became the thing they were best at. Jane's parents agreed.

A year later I was at that same barn, and I heard that my chat with Jane and Remington had been life altering. She did practice in her mind, and then on a course over and over until they became stellar at the water jump. Since then, her confidence in her riding had been soaring, and she was winning everything.

While the victory was great, even better for a young girl with such a passion for horses was that by visualizing and moving her anxiety out of the way, Jane created a deeper bond with Remington and they became a true team. We should all be so diligent about overcoming our fears!

Shifting the Flow

As I mentioned in Chapter 1, many people flock to animal-communication classes hoping to become great receivers of information. At the end of the day, that's only part of it, and it's not even the most dominant or powerful part. Shifting *our* thoughts and feelings can move energy faster than just about any other remedy. Supporting that shift with body or energy work is an efficient way to break up patterns. The first place where we store memories is the body, and this is the last location we release them. Our physical selves should be where we go to work first so that we make room for the thought patterns and emotions to break free.

A first step in starting to become aware of what you're sending is to say "I feel" instead of "I am." If you're feeling something—say, sadness—it's mutable. It's harder to come out of "I *am* sad." Saying that you *feel* angry, rather than that you *are* angry, is also more palatable to others.

For the most part, our animals are more buoyant than we are. We should take full advantage of their cheerfulness . . . especially on the days when that little cynic in all of us wants to answer the phone in the way the writer Dorothy Parker used to: "What fresh hell is this?"

Unquestionably, there are terrible situations that can emotionally scar animals. They do have their own karma, their own histories that have shaped them, but they look to us with a willingness to undo it. They don't blame—they are here, now. If they aren't bouncing out of an emotional state, then something in their human interactions could be blocking the natural progression. It could be as simple as how the previous owner treated them, so then it's our job to break up the patterning—which can involve anything from participating in a joyful activity each day, training, or bodywork, to something as in depth as clearing out old images through energy healing.

One of my favorite scenes in the movie *Babe* is when the pig of the title is very sick. Farmer Hoggett tries bottle-feeding him but is unsuccessful and is at a total loss as to what to do next. All the other farm animals are concerned and desperately try to peer in the window, sure that their hero, Babe, is going to die. Even though Hoggett is bereft and on the verge of breaking down, he starts a jig. He dances fantastically, getting lost in the joy of his kicking movements, and when the song is over, Babe is up and eating his slop.

Even though it's fictional, this is a perfect illustration of how the farmer literally changed the surrounding energy by getting out of that pattern of fear and helplessness. Like a fever breaking, Hogget's jig saved Babe!

Why is it so important to acknowledge our own feelings first? Why is it so critical to then clearly look upon the animals' feelings as independent, viewing them from the observation deck of One Mind? Our feelings, especially when mingled with theirs, can bond them to an experience forever.

For example, if your dog is attacked at the park and you can't let go of the fear and sorrow associated with the incident, something as innocuous as being around other animals can seem life threatening to your pet, and it can very quickly develop into a deep-seated belief system.

Janine and Parker

A woman named Janine came to me with two dogs: an 11-year-old German shepherd and a 4-year-old golden retriever. A few months back they'd lost an eight-year-old Lab that was very dear to the whole gang (including her, her husband, her kids, and the other dogs). She was concerned that the older German shepherd, Parker, wasn't coming out of his grief.

When I connected with Parker, it was clear that he was the overseer of the household. Things weren't going well, and he didn't know how to help. He let me know that nobody in the home had recovered from their grief—the atmosphere was thick with it. He also said that something else was *really* bothering him: The youngest daughter was truly struggling with her homework. The dog sensed that her thoughts were bewildered, as if she were stuck.

Janine was puzzled by this. She agreed that it was true that they'd all mourned an unusually long time over the dog that had passed, but she was baffled by the homework comment. Then she told me about her other children. Two of her kids had been valedictorians of their

41

classes and had received academic scholarships to very fine schools, but her youngest daughter—considered by her mother to be a social butterfly—was still living at home and going to high school. Janine had come to accept that this daughter was probably not as smart as the others. The German shepherd was *not* accepting this.

Janine went home and told her husband. Although he hadn't thought much of the consultation at first, upon hearing this news, he immediately had their daughter tested. They discovered that she was dyslexic, which was preventing her from getting through her homework quickly. This was the bewildering thought process that Parker had clued us in to. The girl, as it turned out, was as smart as her siblings, if not more so for getting as far as she had despite struggling with a learning disability that nobody had caught on to until high school.

Thankfully, Janine had the foresight to see that nobody was coming out of their grief easily and sought help for Parker—and ultimately got help *from* him. Fortunately, the husband took the message seriously. The German shepherd was able to go back to being a hero in the household, and the daughter received the assistance she needed.

Lauren and Jazz

Sometimes we don't recognize how far down we've stuffed our own feelings and what that can do to the household. Lauren called because her cat, Jazz, had an unusually high liver-enzyme count. There seemed to be no apparent reason for this other than the possibility that she had ingested a toxin (Lauren suspected a litter additive). I tuned in, scanning the body first to see if it was a toxin. While it could have been, if so, it was in combination with an emotion that Jazz was holding. In Chinese medicine, the liver represents anger.

I checked in with the cat to see what her relationship was like with each of the other animals in the household. Jazz ran a tight ship, and the other two cats were content to let her rule. One of the dogs regularly blew her off. It annoyed her slightly but didn't really upset her—I knew that wasn't the problem.

Jazz let me know that Lauren was staying home more to manage her teenage son, and it wasn't working out as well as she knew that Lauren had hoped it would. While the boy was doing fine in school, he wasn't grounded emotionally, and his behavior could get out of control in a New York minute. Jazz was picking up on Lauren's frustration at having given up so much. Later I found out from the veterinarian who had referred her to me that Lauren's son indeed had some very big emotional issues to overcome. The vet wasn't the least bit surprised by my findings, and she was able to formulate a plan for Jazz's treatment thereafter.

Commonly an outside toxin—in this case, the litter additive—is able to invade the body when the emotional life of the household is thrown out of balance by someone's anger and frustration. This doesn't just apply to animals, but to us humans, too. There are plenty of otherwise harmless substances we come into contact with every day that can suddenly become dangerous poisons if either our immune system or our emotional life is compromised. Any other time, we could be exposed to the potential toxin and our body would resist it.

Obviously, Lauren and I talked about liver-cleansing ideas, and since she was referred by a vet, I knew that the physical aspect would be in great hands. As far as the household went, I gave her a line I repeat to many people: "Tell the cat that you're handling the situation. Thank her for her concern, and say that you'll take care of it."

To use the words *I have it under control* would be a big fat lie, and the cat would see through it. All it would take is one upsetting episode with the son and Jazz would be even more distressed that she didn't manage the household better. However, saying that she was in the process of "handling" the situation would be true. The more you convey to animals that you're aware of the circumstances, the more likely they are not to worry and buy into the madness. At the end of the day, this statement becomes an affirmation for you as well.

Guilt Won't Help a Thing

If you become aware of how much your choices and behaviors have impacted an animal, it doesn't serve anyone to blame yourself or feel guilty. We're all here in contract with one another. Recognizing that and changing the potential outcome—or seeing what a gift a particular lesson has been—is wonderful. Guilt won't help a thing, as it can create a holding pattern. Feeling bad about the animals' past and how you've conducted your life, thereby impacting them, will make room for a whole lot of unwanted behavior.

A man came to me with his dog, who was moping around because he'd moved from a farm to a home close to the city. As soon as the man released his guilt about the smaller yard, the dog was able to enjoy walking on a leash and other suburban activities. When we have guilt, we're operating from a deficit. Thus, animals could think that they're just busying themselves by digging in the yard or say, "Hey, I'm not doing enough, so I'll just be over here shredding the garbage, thank you very much. Don't mind me."

A woman named Martha and I were in a class together recently. She told me that she was going to have to give up her dog because she felt so guilty that he was in a crate all day while she worked. I said, "Why don't you give up your guilt instead?" She looked at me like I was kooky. A few days later, she told me that she'd followed my advice, and it was amazing. She and the dog had bonded so much. He didn't act like a rambunctious freak when she came home, and the loving relationship between her kids and the animal was rekindled.

Esther and Jerry Hicks work with the great teacher Abraham, a collective voice of ascended masters presented by Esther. One of Abraham's main teachings is that our emotional system is a guidepost, so to speak, pointing out whether we're in alignment with our spirit or not. Once we're aware of this, we can simply do things—whether through exercise, prayer, or even something fun—in order to move on up the ladder to a more joyous state and get back in alignment. Oftentimes those little loving creatures in our homes with eyes staring up at us are just the reminder we need that it's time to break up the holding pattern and play with a string toy or walk around the block and get out of a particular mood or frame of mind, even just for a few minutes.

The Importance of Words

Being crystal clear about the specific words you choose is imperative: Say what you mean and mean what you say. Words are usually the second thing people become conscious of when learning this work.

Once I was at a horse show talking to the animals. A woman followed me around, wanting to sign her horse up for a chat, yet she kept telling me that she didn't believe in what I was doing. I certainly don't have time to convince anyone of anything, so I continued on my way even though she was shadowing me. Eventually, she told me how she'd picked up her dog after having to amputate his leg due to cancer, and she'd just gotten on the freeway when loud and clear in her head she heard: *Why did you let them take my leg?* She said that she had to pull over.

That was a telepathic scream. Not all of us have heard such resounding words. Sometimes during psychic experiences or our first time out of the chute with energy work, we get scared; we back away from that which we don't understand. But many of us have picked up on words from a dog about going on a walk, from a cat about a litter box being dirty, or from a horse saying that today we should jump—and we think that it's *our* idea. The animals are just relieved that *finally* we've heard them. Probably over half of our behavior is influenced by them, and they think that we're really smart because we're getting it at last!

Henry was a mutt, possibly with miniature poodle or bichon frise genes. In any event, he was 18 pounds of cuteness . . . a three-year-old stray who came into his human guardian's life shortly after she'd lost two larger dogs—a black Lab and a wheaten terrier—to old age. Having such a small animal was a new experience for her, and she responded by treating Henry a bit like a toy, speaking in baby talk and demanding that he snuggle with her on the sofa. Her feelings were hurt when Henry, although sometimes affectionate, often responded aggressively and even nipped her on occasion. One day when they were sitting quietly together, she clearly heard the words: *I'm not a baby—I'm a man.* The hair stood up on the back of her neck.

She had known that despite his size, this was indeed a macho guy (he often reared up and walked on his back legs with a swagger in the presence of larger dogs), yet it hadn't occurred to her that he might resent being called "Mommy's little snuggle-bunny" in public! She changed her tone and the words she used with him to almost immediate effect. When he was addressed as an adult and given the task of keeping an eye on the house while she was away, Henry became calmer and no longer got in her face and showed his teeth when she tried to pet him . . . but he did cuddle up on her lap on his own terms and when no one else was around!

When communicating with animals, I can tell when someone has been telling them over and over again how good or beautiful they are. One dog repeatedly told me, "I am so handsome." It turned out that his person did constantly tell him just how handsome he was.

People sometimes want copies of my notes, which really look like babble. I quickly scribble them down to expound upon, but frequently they look like this: "I'm a good dog. I love the smells in the yard. The woman was wrecked over her breakup. I'm a good dog. I have a lot of dog friends. I'm a good dog. I liked our old house better. I'm a good dog." I do write down every time the animal says "I'm a good dog," because obviously these are words that are sticking, and the person should be acknowledged for giving the dog positive affirmations.

If you suddenly hear a word pop into your head when you're in a quiet, receptive state of mind, it's probably coming from an outside source. You might be getting a transmitted picture from your animal, and you as a human have the words to complete it. For instance, a dog may be sending a picture of the leash and you hear *leash* because that's how your mind works. In my classes, people who are writers, lawyers, advertisers, and so on tend to pick up on words first.

Susan and Tory

On the occasions when I only hear one word repeatedly, I know that there's something much bigger going on that the animal is protecting. I went to a barn in the Seattle area where a horse, Tory, wouldn't stay in the stall and would flip out when confined. When I got there, he was out in a paddock and seemed relaxed.

I asked him why he didn't want to remain in his stall. He kept repeating, "Murder." Murder? Who or what was murdered? Did it happen in a stall? I asked a thousand questions. Nothing. At this point I was feeling pretty dumb. Could it be that an animal in the stall next to him was euthanized? What could this mean?

The Sheriff with Deputy Megan.

I asked Susan, the guardian, why Tory might be saying this word. She was stunned. It turns out that at a barn where the horse was boarded years before, there was a trainer whom he loved. She had cancer and was undergoing treatment. Prior to her diagnosis, she was planning to get divorced. The husband decided to stay with her during her treatment, and they were supposedly working out their problems.

Then the trainer was found dead, facedown in the horse pasture—she had drowned in a puddle. The story was that she was so weak from chemotherapy that she must have fallen and drowned. Susan and several others suspected that the husband killed her and set it up to look like an accident. The horse was greatly relieved when I told this story, because the mystery surrounding the untimely death of the trainer left unanswered questions for the people around her. The trainer's death was never tried as a murder case, but it gave peace to Susan and Tory that the story was out.

As if that weren't enough, Tory witnessed another terrible scene across the street from the barn where he was next boarded, and this time it was *definitely* murder. He saw a woman run out of a door screaming "Help!" She was pulled back in again, and then there was a gunshot. Tory is an Arabian: too smart for his own good. He could do nothing about either of these situations.

Tory shared more routine thoughts about his physical well-being and other matters after the murder revelations, but needless to say, he never moved back into a stall. He required a centrally located paddock, where he could see all the comings and goings and scream if something were to go wrong. Everyone at the barn had a new understanding of how Tory was looking out for everyone. He was no longer perceived as a neurotic horse but as a hero. People reverentially named him "The Sheriff." All the other horses were his deputies.

Julie and Hank

I came to a dressage barn in Los Angeles to talk to a horse named Hank who was a weaver, which means he stood with his head outside the stall, swinging it back and forth—a somewhat neurotic behavior. In addition, he wasn't performing up to his usual standards at horse shows anymore. He kept shifting away from me and saying, "I'm the funny guy. I'm the funny guy. I'm the funny guy." I was sweating bullets trying to get more from him than that. Flat line. Nothing. *Nada.* So finally I told his guardian, Julie, that she had a Jim Carrey of a horse. She looked at me like I had two heads and announced emphatically, "There is *nothing* funny about him."

Okay, then I got it: She was humorless. So I suggested that maybe Hank understood something about her that he wasn't going to share with me in order to protect her, but perhaps it was along the lines of saying that she should lighten up and have a good time while she was riding.

That didn't go over so well either. I asked what she did with him, and Julie gave me a description of their very rigid working habits. Basically, Hank told me the same thing. They had a strict warm-up and then an utterly predictable set of exercises to complete. It became the same thing day after day. He was bored to tears.

I suggested, "Well, I'd tell him a joke every day when you ride or go on the trail." Now Julie thought that I was truly nuts. At that point, what do you do? Personally, if nothing else was working, I think that I'd try the joke. Again, I'm not in the business of convincing; I'm in the business of *connecting*. She wasn't going to hear it then. Once in a while you come across occasions when even though folks call you, they don't really want the help—at least not at that moment. Maybe some part of them heard what you said, maybe not . . . but I can't think about it once I've gone; I can only hope and leave it at that.

I ran into Julie's trainer on the way out, and she asked me what I got from the horse. I said that the only thing I picked up on was that he was a repressed funny guy, but his rider wouldn't lighten up. The trainer concurred with me that this was the whole problem.

Months later, I was riding out on the trail, and this same unfunny woman flew by me on that same funny-guy horse. She was going fast with a huge smile on her face—I hardly recognized her. As she passed, she said, "I've been meaning to call and thank you. And now I need you to talk to my bird."

Sometimes the animal won't let me in on the whole story. A dog once told me, "I like to go on the walks that no other dogs get to go on." He was referring to the other canine members of the household. Well, as it turns out, he had a sneaky way of getting out of his yard, but the owner never believed that he was out snooping through the neighborhood while she was at work. On a weekly basis she got calls from neighbors saying that the dog was in their yard. She really couldn't believe it because he was so well behaved. To back up her belief, she used to go home after she'd get a call, and magically the dog would be sitting in his spot in the kitchen with the two others.

One day she got smart. She came home and checked on the dog—as always, he was where he was supposed to be. Before she went back to work that day, however, she parked her car up the street. Sure enough, about three minutes after she turned off her engine, her dog came sneaking around the corner. Of course, he refused to tell me *how* he was getting out!

Recently, in a phone session, a notoriously feisty cat let me know that no matter how happy-go-lucky her person was out in the world, deep down, "She's every bit as tough a broad as I am!"

A menacing but not quite aggressive dog once told me, "Nobody gets my humor."

Ultimately, words are the agent for thoughts or feelings. Even by choosing to change them, we can affect our mental and emotional state. For example, if you say that a dog has a problem, then he will forever have one. How about instead saying that this dog has a "challenge"?

A challenge is much easier to overcome than a problem.

If I tell my dog that I have to write or finish phone sessions before we do something together, she mopes around. But if I tell her to create her own "dog day" while I'm working and then at 4 o'clock we get to go have fun, it's a whole different ball game: She's out monitoring the yard!

Pictures Are Key

Believe it or not, the pictures we hold on to can create the biggest imaginable breakdown in communication. Feelings and words can fuel that failure, but the pictures we cling to signal whether we're aware of what we're transmitting or not.

Let's say for a moment that your cat peed on the new rug. You're mad and upset, but then you feel guilty for being angry because maybe, just maybe, there's something wrong with your poor beloved kitty. You take her to the vet and the blood work comes back 100 percent perfect—there's nothing physically wrong with her. As a result, you're *really* mad, confused, and hurt. You go to the store and buy a cleaning product to take out the cat-pee smell. You're upset because you'd finally been able to afford that new rug. You're also glad because the cat's blood work was fine.

But even more than being unhappy about the rug, you're upset because the cat has, to some degree, betrayed you. At the very least, she has broken the code of honor in your household. Now the images your thoughts are transmitting are going between *cat, rug, cat, rug, upset, rug, cat, rug, upset, cat, rug.* . . . The cat knows that you're upset, *and* she's being bombarded with pictures of the rug. You're now accidentally sending energetic arrows saying, "Please pee here on the rug."

Just in that paragraph alone, how many times did you picture a cat and/or a rug, and how often did you visualize a cat *peeing* on a rug? The cat knows that you're upset but doesn't understand why, nor does she know the value of the rug. However, the images you're sending are so strong that she thinks perhaps it would please you if she peed on the rug.

In situations where you feel yourself getting upset, *know that whether you like it or not, pictures are flying out! And the more upset you are, the more you broadcast.* It's better to cancel the thought of the rug and replace it with an image of the litter box. In fact, if you know that it really bothers you, post a picture of a litter box at your desk at work or on the fridge, and start retraining your mind.

Every animal communicator probably uses the following story, but it illustrates this point so well. You tell a dog in big, loud words to get off the couch, and when he does, you say, "Good dog." But then you think, *When I leave the room, he's going to get right back on the couch.* What's the dog going to do? Of course, immediately and with purpose, he'll resume his position on the sofa. So many of us are sending mixed messages all the time.

Another example is aggressive dogs. In such a case, I'm the first person to say, "Don't call me—call a dog trainer." People always want to know why I would recommend that. They're curious why their dog is aggressive. The "why" at this point hardly matters. The "what" needs to be addressed for the safety of the dog's guardian and others. Usually people are still committed to finding out the details. Sometimes this does help the training process, but for the most part, a good dog trainer will know how to handle the situation and educate the person appropriately.

I'll give an example of one client in Los Angeles, but this is very common. A woman had a dog who used to become aggressive toward other dogs while he was on a leash during walks outside. (She claimed that he wasn't hostile off a leash.) They lived in a very urban area where practically everyone emptied out onto the street in the morning to walk their dogs. Since the woman was a professional, the only times she had available to take her dog out were when everyone else was also doing it, so clearly this was a problem.

Every dog has a different story that relates to the emotional charge underlying the cause of aggression. So the psychic end of what I got from that specific dog made no difference—more important was what was happening every time the woman walked outside with him. She clung to an image of an instance when he had attacked another dog—he'd actually gone for the throat. The trauma of it all remained etched in her brain. That picture was so locked in that it changed her body language, which now exuded fear. Her voice sounded strained. This confident career woman's shoulders would suddenly droop, and she would clutch the leash. The dog experienced her insecurity because she was no longer in charge and was grasping for a solution. Lo and behold, the picture of the dog going for a throat was cemented, and *voilà*—the dog went for the first victim he could find *because he was sure that he was supposed to do this in order to help her.*

The woman and I worked with a dog trainer, strengthened her vocal authority, and built up her physical stature.

All three of those things helped so that no matter what picture flashed through her mind, meeting other dogs was a more balanced event—even a positive endeavor.

Nick and Lucy

The mixed pictures we send don't always result in threatening, snarling teeth or the irritating smell of cat urine after a long day at work. The story of Lucy is rather endearing.

Lucy's guardian, Nick, flung open the door before I could even knock. He had his baby in a pouch in front of him and a piece of paper in hand. He ushered me into the living room, where his wife sat with the dog. They had a two-page typed list of what they wanted her to know and what they hoped to ask her . . . so we got to work. They were primarily concerned that since the arrival of the human baby, Lucy didn't feel loved or was jealous.

Neither of those things applied to Lucy. She knew that she was valued and cherished. She was a little overwhelmed by the crying and the baby smells sometimes, but her position as the *dog* certainly wasn't rattled by an infant. The couple confirmed that she didn't seem envious; they just wanted to make sure.

Finally, Nick asked me about the fact that Lucy shook sometimes when she got up close to the baby. The dog showed me that they'd told her repeatedly about the coming little one. They always referred to their friends' kids, telling Lucy that the baby would be like them. But those children were toddler sized and bigger. Lucy was expecting a toddler—something much larger than a newborn—to appear. Instead, here was this unpredictable, frighteningly vulnerable little creature all wrapped up. It was frankly a bit overwhelming at times, unless he was asleep. Accidentally, the couple had sent the wrong picture.

Nick and his wife just couldn't believe it—all of their friends did have older kids, and that's the story they had repeatedly told Lucy: "It will be like Lily or Faith." We helped the dog understand that eventually this baby *would* be that size and then get bigger and bigger. Lucy became even better at watching the baby after that!

Familiar Scenes

Just to break it down even more, it's not as if we have a full-stream video called "Joan's Life: Unplugged" for anyone who's adept at telepathy to see! Rather, it can be a simple image or series of images. Pictures stick—they become like files stored in the brain.

In my early 20s, I did a play by Edward Albee called *Seascape.* (Yes, I was in the role of Sarah the lizard for those of you who know it.) When you're working in theater, there's the rehearsal time, there's the performance, and then there's the piece's shelf life. By that I mean that the characters, the emotions, and the thoughts that underlie the play stay in your system much longer than the duration of its run—even, in fact, after you've moved on and done several others.

Two years after I'd finished *Seascape,* with many other intervening pieces, I was visiting a friend in Montauk, New York. Early the first morning, I walked down on the beach, and the entire landscape was familiar to me even though I'd never been there. When I came back up for breakfast and explained my experience to my friend, she said, "Oh, Edward Albee lives two doors down." He'd written the play from that house.

Many times when I've had a phone session with someone and then years later have done an in-home consultation, the whole setting will seem familiar, as if images of it were sent by the animal.

I did a series of phone sessions with a woman named Jacquie. She ran a rehab center for horses in Montana, and we went over the needs of all those she'd acquired and was bringing back to health. An obvious next step for her was to learn animal communication, so she arranged for me to come and teach in her town. I'd never seen a picture of Jacquie through the entire period of working with her, yet when I got off the plane, I knew immediately who she was in the crowd.

When I started taking this work seriously, I realized pretty early on that my personal weakness was pictures. I could get a whole story from the animals, it seemed, from the words and the feelings—in fact, they all came very fast (just as images do). I worked very diligently at slowing down the whole process and really trying to get visuals as I was going along. Eventually, I realized how much of our imagination is fed by pictures from people and other sources around us, and they come quite readily now. They'd always been there; they'd always come that easily, but because my brain wasn't thinking in that way, I wasn't aware of them.

As people tell us a story, we see images. Every time *we* tell one, we're also passing along images. Just as a fun exercise when you're chatting on the phone with a friend or are talking to someone at work, tune in through the pictures as well. It's a great way not only to listen with awareness, but also to develop that telepathic muscle.

When we're beginning, we may see images in the form of shapes. Sometimes I still get bizarre ones, and I don't hesitate to ask the client what they might be, as it will further the process of getting to the animal's needs. Here's a great example that I use in my classes all the time.

Audrey had moved from New York City to Los Angeles with her four cats and had me over to see if they were settling into their new abode. She also wanted to know if they needed anything from her, as she was about to start acupuncture school and her time would be limited. We had a very nice session and got to all of their needs. At the end, Audrey asked me what the cats missed the most about New York. One of them showed me this thick, white shape. I didn't know what the heck it was, so I just said, "Your cat is showing me this white wavy thing."

Audry started laughing and then said, "Oh" in a feeling-sad-out-loud sort of way. Apparently she'd had an old futon with the bottom ripped out, and the cat had liked to get in there and sleep on the white wavy stuffing. Audrey had thrown out the futon when she moved from New York.

When playing telepathic games using mental images involving a specific color, the receiving partner will often get *apple* when the sender is transmitting *heart*. We can decipher shapes with practice and in context. However, in the beginning, if you do get a picture that even remotely has the same form as something being sent to you, feel free to jump up and down with excitement, because that's awesome.

Some artists actually get pictures easily. Those with highly acute visual senses often receive them immediately. For the most part, though, people tend to get feelings first, words second, and pictures last.

Lost Animals

Pictures are particularly important in lost-animal cases, which for me are the hardest part of being an animal communicator. Locating a lost cat or dog is like trying to find a needle in a haystack. At times, the client and I will be a day or even just hours behind the animal. The person will go to the place I've identified, and somebody will have just seen the pet, but alas, the bewildered animal has continued on in an attempt to get home. Many animals lose their built-in navigational system for a number of reasons:

1. The emotions surrounding being lost, such as fear and sadness, to name a couple

2. A barometric-pressure change that not only switches around their own chemistry for the moment, but also changes the smells in the atmosphere

3. Adrenalin if they were chased away by something or someone (for dogs it takes ten hours for their adrenalin levels to return to normal)

Probably the most important of the three is the emotional component. The person and the animal may have so much fear or sadness about the event that neither is seeing clearly. A dog or cat could be three doors down and so confused that it takes days or weeks before the animal figures that fact out, so having a neutral party involved in order to get the images about their location helps.

Unfortunately, in many cases, it becomes something deeper than "Where are you now?" When an animal isn't found, it can become a lesson in unresolved closure. Every lost-animal scenario is different.

Christine and Marco

A woman named Christine in Michigan had taken her cat, Marco, to the vet. While in the office, a dog had scared him just as someone was coming through the door, and the cat seized the opportunity and ran out. Marco was timid and had never been outside. To make matters worse, being a house cat, he had no tags. When it came to finding him, let's just move this one into the impossibility zone by mentioning the fact that the vet's office was on the edge of a giant city park.

I knew nothing of this area when I asked Marco where he was. He showed me that there was a golf course—or some sort of a green stretch—and in one direction was a large cement bin with garbage stored inside. He'd stationed himself between that and a small patch of woods. Straight ahead opposite the garbage bin was what seemed to be a very large two-story home with a veranda around it, and it appeared that there was a party there every night, as though it could have been a restaurant.

This was a mammoth park, and it took Christine many days, maybe even a week, to find the right area. Once she located this particular restaurant, she staked out the big garbage bin and left food nearby. This went on for months. I usually stay neutral and try not to add my own pain to the equation of what both the human and animal are feeling in their attempt to reunite. But as time went on, I became really disappointed by how hard we were trying without gaining any more information.

Christine was aware of all the feral cats in the area, yet she somehow *knew* that they weren't the ones eating her food—she was sure that Marco was around. Park officials thought that they'd seen him but couldn't be positive. That was enough for her to keep going back. She was also aware that her cat was just too cautious to reveal himself in this uncharted territory.

Months later, I saw something different: Near the patch of woods there appeared to be a safe zone where there were some big, beautiful older homes. Christine started putting flyers up in that neighborhood. After a month, someone responded who had left food out for their own outdoor cat and had seen hers on their deck.

Now Christine was elated, but still it was weeks before I heard from her again. Frankly, I was exhausted by the situation and had never seen anything like this woman's tenacity. I believe this went on for about six months altogether. I almost didn't pick up the phone that day, as I was late getting out to my own horses. When I did, she asked me if I would please tell her one more thing, any little bit of information that could tip her off.

All I could see was a tiny gravel pathway down to a cellar door. Even the gravel was small, more like pebbles. On either side was lattice with chipped paint. So

Christine went back to the neighborhood where the cat was spotted and walked through backyards until she found a location that matched my description. I usually tell people that if you find one place that seems to fit the bill but doesn't pan out, keep trying. Always expand your search. Christine sat there calling her cat . . . for an hour. She had given up and was just about to leave when she heard a meow. At long last, she found her cat's secret hideout. Christine called me that afternoon with Marco safe at home, where he sat and purred and purred.

When a Picture Tells a Story

One day I was at a barn working with a trainer and her horses and clients. She was having the most trouble with a tall, striking thoroughbred. He was very athletic, yet he didn't like to jump. The horse showed me how he'd crumpled out of a starting gate once, and that's how he wounded his right hind leg. I didn't know at the time that the trainer didn't believe me, as there was no indication of an injury.

She called the original owner and was told that yes, the horse *had* had a terrible accident at the racetrack: He'd gotten his right hind leg stuck in the starting gate. The former owner then sent the x-rays, which explained why he didn't want to jump. The rest of this story gets better. The trainer was more careful around the leg with this knowledge . . . yet the horse still didn't want to jump. So about two years later, I bought him—and we don't jump!

Countless times when I visit a couple, one person is more skeptical. I'll just say it—usually it's the husband.

He keeps his mouth shut and hangs out in the doorway with his arms crossed, ready to doubt every tidbit of information I give them. In the end, arms unfolded, he joins us and says that the story the dog told me was just what he's imagined, or he confirms for me that the situation I've revealed is true. So many times the husband will say, "That's exactly what I pictured." Even the most skeptical will admit to seeing images as I'd described them.

Meanwhile, the husband may go back to the office the next day and say that his wife just wasted their money—that's if he even admits that an animal communicator came over. Deep in his heart, though, ultimately I confirmed for him that he had a profound communication with his beloved animal.

Clever Hans and Rico

Clever Hans was a horse in the early 1900s in Germany who could do mathematical equations—at least, so it seemed. His owner gave him brainy (for a horse!) little arithmetic tasks such as: "If today is Tuesday, how many days until Sunday?" By tapping with his hoof, Clever Hans would count it out. People were astounded by this and came in droves to watch.

Then other folks tried to set up the equations to test him. Clever Hans's owner was a math teacher and would have had math embedded in his thought patterns, seeping out of his cells. Sadly, Clever Hans was not able to perform the same feat for other testers, and it was assumed that he was actually reading the subtle body language of his owner. It was disappointing to all the crowds who came from miles and miles around to see him, but Clever Hans was also so deeply disappointed that he was known for biting his testers!

On the other hand, more recently at the Max Planck Institute for Evolutionary Anthropology in Leipzig, Germany, researchers have been studying a border collie named Rico whose people brought him there because he knew up to 200 simple words. Rico averages picking up 37 out of 40 items correctly. And he can even give them to specific people. Many tests were conducted to make sure that this was not another Clever Hans.

Rico has proven that there is reasoning at work in animals. When presented with an unfamiliar object, the dog can immediately identify it in association with a new word. Clever Hans illustrated that relationship is everything. Imagine being one of those doubters and feeling so proud that you disproved this big horse's ability, and then Clever Hans sinks his teeth right into your arm like it was a bright, shiny apple. He knew he was being doubted—and how annoying is that!?

Through the example of Clever Hans, scientists were able to discern a lot about the human/animal relationship, and they're learning quite a bit about how dogs reason through Rico. Both cases involve images being passed back and forth. Clever Hans was so in tune with his person that he was able to read him like a book. Rico's family discovered that he knew many words before he was brought to the Institute. In both instances, the animals were pleaser types (in Clever Hans's case, maybe only for his person and an *open-minded* crowd who wanted to be amazed). The intelligence displayed here is huge.

There are many ways animals in our own homes are tracking situations. They do so with their senses, of course. They watch for body language, and they hear the cadence with which we speak—a different tone will alert them if something's up. But make no mistake—they're also tracking the images in our minds.

❖ ❖ ❖ ❖

❖ Chapter Four ❖

LESSONS FROM ANIMALS

*The wind of Heaven is that which
blows between a horse's ears.*
— Arabian proverb

Every now and again, someone will approach me at an event where I'm speaking or presenting and feel compelled to tell me that they also do animal-communication work, but that what they do is far more "spiritual."

I hold back my immediate smart-ass response because it won't serve either of us, and I just say, "Good for you— thank you for sharing." The reason I bring this up (and reveal my own character flaw!) is that to me, *all* animal communication is connected to Spirit. For me, there are no words to describe the peace I feel after a great horse-back ride.

Having all of our animals in harmony *is* heavenly. Creating a space where the beings in our home are fully expressing themselves yet living within the boundaries of acceptable behavior is what we're all striving for. If we can have a little piece of bliss at home, we can go out and *be* that in the world.

One very cold, wet morning I was working at a barn in the Seattle area. As I drove up, people were signing up with the horse trainer for a session with me. A woman approached me, told me that she was third on the list, and then somewhat challengingly announced, "I've had several sessions with this other animal communicator, and we've discovered that my horse and I have had six past lives together."

"Great. Did it stop the bucking?" I asked.

"No," she replied, surprised.

"Well, that's what we'll work on today then."

Honeyhorse's Dirty Trick

I know a thing or two about bucking! That was courtesy of my second childhood horse, Honeyhorse, who truly taught me how to ride. During the late-fall to midwinter period after I first got her—a muddy, gray, cloudy time—I was learning Western riding. (When I was 12, I got my first jumping saddle and haven't ridden Western much since.) Now Honeyhorse could be a great little mare with the trainer and when it came time for a lesson, but she definitely knew how to throw a curveball.

On days when I wasn't in a lesson, the indoor arena seemed small and claustrophobic with all of those other after-school riders. Across the way from the barn where I kept Honeyhorse was the entrance to a big public arena where horse shows took place in the spring and summer. Everything, including crossing the busy street, would go fine as I rode over there on Honeyhorse, and all went well when we first entered the arena.

However, on the far side from the entrance was a giant puddle that remained all winter long. Honeyhorse's trick was to buck me off into this muddy pool. After I got up, it would take me a while to catch her. I would then lead her back to the barn, all the while trying to figure out the problem: Was it the puddle? Was it me? Was she mean? What if I went the other way? Was there a bogey-man off in the distant woods that spooked her?

My mother would be at the barn waiting to pick me up, and I wouldn't say a word because if I did, she could very well sell Honeyhorse back to the trainer. I *knew* that I couldn't handle this horse, but it didn't occur to me that I might address the problem with the trainer. Frankly, I didn't want to come off as the novice that I was. If anyone asked me why I was so muddy, I'd just say that we had to splash through a million puddles. I knew how to cover up the abuse!

Believe it or not, this was our pattern for months. Both of us expected it. For her it was a game . . . it was fun. As for me, I couldn't believe that I was duped again—I wouldn't acknowledge that I didn't have great balance. Meanwhile, I was unaware of my participation in setting myself up to be bucked off the moment I walked into the arena and could see the puddle at the far end.

Then one day, as if the clouds parted and the sun came shining through, we were trotting around the far side and Honeyhorse bucked—but I held on. Wow! I made a circle and trotted through the puddle and stayed on a second time. Incredible. I never came off of her again in that arena. She even stopped bucking at that spot.

We were amazing partners from then on for years and years. Of course, she had other shenanigans, but by then I was amused by them—except for the first time we were in a jumping class in a horse show. We did our warm-up circle, and she leaped right out of the entrance gate instead of doing the course. Needless to say, we were disqualified, but Honeyhorse never did that again. She had picked up on how nervous I was and took full advantage. I did come off one other time six years later, but that was because I unknowingly built a mini-jump course over a wasps' nest. *That* was my fault!

Communication Setbacks

When people have been hurt or scared by their horse, I look for four things:

1. I search through the horse's personality to see if the animal is naughty, defensive, fearful, or has a mean streak.

2. I also examine the horse's physical body to determine if the behavior is caused by pain.

3. I then look at the equipment—does it fit properly?

4. Then I notice the rider's communication method—is he or she giving a wrong cue, or is this a mental miscommunication?

With hindsight, I now know that I'd been mentally setting myself up with Honeyhorse by holding the expectation that she'd buck and I'd fall. She was continually testing me. Once I stayed on, I then had *that* expectation.

We could trot, canter, walk, stop in the mud puddle, and then just breeze through. I never looked back, because I was so excited about where we could go from there.

All animals to some degree, but especially horses, ask us to assert who we are, and they'll push the envelope in order to find out who *they* are. We all know a little more about ourselves in relation to others by coming up against obstacles. As animals go along in a pack or herd, they push one another until they discover where they are in the pecking order. So it's normal for them to test us a bit and see what we're made of.

When scary horse behavior goes beyond this, I keep digging to see what else could be causing it. If the problem is equipment not fitting well, that's an easy fix. It could be that a saddle should be looked at. The equipment should be working with you to *enhance* communication, not hinder it. More often than not, though, it's physical pain. Sometimes an old injury has crept back in—and again, this is changeable. It could be that teeth need to be checked or the horse just needs a massage or a chiropractic adjustment.

I recently went to a stable to help a rider with her horse. The woman told me that he kicked out when she asked him to canter in one direction. I first checked in with the horse's physical body, and while he had some aches, they weren't enough to warrant that reaction. Then I asked him about the rider. He let me know that she was not only timid, but she also wasn't following his movements. And he was very talented, was well trained, and had natural rhythm! He told me that when she gave a cue for a different gait, she wasn't balanced and leaned on one side. Plus, she made demands with too much "oomph."

His kicking out was basically him saying, "Hello! I got it." Switching into another gait with a well-balanced horse *and* rider should be like shifting gears in a Ferrari . . . these two were more like bumper cars. I ran into the woman a few weeks later, and she said that she was sitting straighter on the horse, following his rhythm, and learning to be a stronger rider. She took the information to heart, and this had really enhanced their communication.

Our physical selves follow our minds, whether we like it or not. This is true with animals, too, as they frequently read our body language. Fear can show up in our physical stature quickly, and that can lead to a reaction from the animal.

Kirsten, Venus, and Frank

Physical stature and standing strong aren't just important with horses, dogs, and cats; birds can react to our fear and timidity as much as any other animal. A woman named Kirsten called me for a session about her two birds. One of them, Venus, had been her best friend for many years, but Kirsten thought she needed a bird companion, so she got Frank, a young rascal of a guy.

Well, all hell broke loose in the house. Venus started screaming and plucking out her feathers. Frank was so cute that everyone loved him and went to his cage immediately, but he took to biting Kirsten and her husband. While Frank was adorable, precious, and entertaining at a distance, he couldn't be trusted at close quarters.

When Kirsten called me, she was beside herself. She hated seeing Venus this unhappy, and she was heartsick over the idea of giving up Frank. When I checked in with Venus, it was clear to me that although she was in a bigger cage, Frank had a higher perch. On occasion, Venus was secretly amused by the other bird, but he was such a big show-off that most of the time she was just disgusted with him. Plus, Venus felt that Frank had no respect for her.

When I checked in with Frank, he was very smart and full of himself and had the whole house wired. He could even control the dog from his high vantage point. Life was grand for Frank. I'm not sure at what age birds come into their hormones, but basically he was like a teenage boy on a Friday night with the keys to Dad's sports car. He did like to poke fun at Venus, and while he loved Kirsten and her husband, he had their number, too. Feeding became a game. In addition, Kirsten had a demure voice, so that didn't help matters.

Kirsten and I discussed what the birds had to say and how similar in personality she and Venus were. They were both lovely spirits, and that was what was making Venus's screaming and plucking even more alarming. Up until then, she'd been very even-keeled. Finally, because I had the sense that Frank loomed over everyone, I asked Kirsten her height. She told me that she was about 5'2". I inquired where Frank's perch was, and she said that it was positioned very high to make up for the fact that his cage was smaller.

Since Kirsten was so fearful of being bitten again, I suggested that she lower Frank's perch. I also recommended that she get a little step she could stand on so that she towered over the bird. We also talked about how to help Venus still feel like "number one."

I didn't hear back from Kirsten until about a year later. On that occasion I had a full day of phone sessions, and

I remember thinking that one of the names on the list looked familiar. When the appointment time came, the phone rang and it was Kirsten. I opened up the picture on the computer and saw Frank's photo. I immediately said to Kirsten, "You never moved the perch."

Kirsten responded, "No, I can't believe you remember that."

"I'm not doing another phone session with you until you do move it," I told her, "because there's nothing the birds are going to tell me that would make as big a difference as that." I got off the phone and didn't charge for the session.

Three weeks later, I received an e-mail from Kirsten saying that after our conversation, she lowered the perch, and everything had changed from that very day on. Venus stopped screaming and plucking her feathers out. Frank ceased biting, Kirsten could let him out in the house, and she didn't fear for her life when she fed him. While he demanded a lot of attention, he'd finally become very sweet and affectionate. She even said that he and Venus were kind of flirting! At last the whole household wasn't captive to Frank's antics.

When things get derailed in our own homes, it's a message and an opportunity to get back on track. This doesn't mean that you have to criticize or judge your own actions; rather, step outside of yourself for a second, look objectively, and start afresh. Some people love their animals so much and do everything they can to make things better, yet they feel like a hostage to the situation at hand.

I love it when people say that they want things to "go back to normal." First of all, what *is* normal? Second, what is going back? Every moment is an opportunity to breathe and adjust, a chance to tune in to One Mind for the objectivity to address the situation. Emotionally charged scenarios frequently lead to bad decisions, so the more you can step back, the better you can serve the highest good of all involved.

Suzanne and Magic

A barn owner asked me to talk to several horses and their various owners. Suzanne, the last woman of the day, stands out in particular.

As I'm getting the name, breed, age, and so forth, I always ask the owners if they feel that their horse is having a behavioral problem or experiencing a physical limitation, or if they want a general reading. Suzanne told me that Magic was having a behavioral issue, but she didn't want to disclose what it was. Some people like to tell me up front; some don't. It makes no difference to me.

When I checked in with the mare, she seemed very sweet. She liked her work, but there were bodily issues that were very hard for her. She was balking (that is, stopping) and on occasion had to rear. I continued by telepathically scanning her body. Her withers (the ridges above the shoulders) were locked. This was originally due to an injury in the right hind foot, but now the problem was exacerbated by an ill-fitting saddle. Mind you, the horse was in the corner of her stall the whole time eating her hay, her feet covered by thick shavings. I hadn't even taken a look at her yet, nor had I touched the withers.

I told Suzanne about Magic's personality, and she agreed with my assessment. I asked if the behavioral problem was balking and rearing, and she confirmed that it was. Then as I was about to proceed to the body, she stopped me, adamantly saying that there was nothing physically wrong with the horse—she was perfectly sound.

I said, "Well, something happened about two years ago to the right hind foot, and there's either soft-tissue damage or scar tissue that's inhibiting her from putting her full weight on it."

"Oh no!" Suzanne exclaimed defiantly.

I continued, saying that the imbalance traveled to the right hip and shortened the shoulder. I was able to poke and show Suzanne that the ribs were out of alignment and that the left side was completely compensating. This horse had a desire to be a beautiful dressage horse, yet her body couldn't support it.

"She's sound" was the owner's mantra.

Finally, Suzanne's friend piped up: "Isn't that the foot she kicked through the wall?"

Suzanne then told me that most of the horse's hoof came off on that occasion, and it took quite some time to grow back. Then she admitted that the saddle didn't fit properly.

When Suzanne pulled Magic out of the stall, I tried a little stretch with her withers; they didn't move. I showed Suzanne exactly where the saddle was cutting off the horse's circulation and why she was rearing. But she just continued saying, "She's sound." She added, "Once you get her working, she's okay."

I explained that in the wild, horses (or any animal) would have to wall off pain for survival. If they're hurt but something frightened them, they could run for hours. Now their biggest survival issue is whether or not we like them. Magic adored Suzanne and wanted to do the right thing. She wasn't going to engage her whole body until she finally loosened up in the shoulders, the saddle wasn't strangling her, and she believed that the foot wasn't going to hurt.

Then Suzanne said that if she was really gentle with the horse in the cross ties, it was even worse out in the ring. I said, "How do you know she isn't thinking that very thing: *Oh, my person is being so sweet—she must finally get how painful this is?* And then you hop on her back with this ill-fitting saddle." Both human and horse felt betrayed.

By chance, at this point in the battle I happened to look down at Magic's right hind foot. Lo and behold, the coronet band—the line between the leg and hoof—sloped down (it should be straight). I could also see where the foot was worn down on one half.

I said, "This is a pet psychic's dream: actual visual proof. You need x-rays, a chiropractor, and a saddle fitter. Furthermore, you quite possibly have the worst farrier in town." (I may have used some adult language while conveying this!)

If people need to be right, God bless them. Some actually learn by being defensive. Even though they're saying no, no, and more no, with any luck—deep in the back of their minds—other ideas have taken seed. From what the horse and Suzanne told me, prior to all this madness, they'd been a dynamic team. I could only hope that they would get back on track.

It was their journey—and for me, that day it was part of mine to remember that all people are where they are.

Even if the woman was mad at me (and I honestly don't care about that), eventually the horse would get some help. And in fact, while on a walk days later, Suzanne did become aware of how hard it was for Magic to use her full body.

Thoughts Are Things

When you have an unconstructive mental loop going, you may be creating disempowering feelings to support your thought pattern. It has control of you. Look around—it may have control of *more* than just you. Thoughts crystallize into form faster than you know.

A woman named Theresa called me over to do a session with her dog, who was misbehaving in the show ring. When I got there, I met a very sweet golden retriever. Not only was this champion dog completely sabotaging the competitions, she was now shredding things in the household.

"This is so unlike her—she wasn't even this bad as a puppy," a distraught Theresa told me. When I tuned in to the dog, she seemed very happy and normal and had no explanation for her behavior. However, she told me that Theresa had failed at an "enterprise."

I asked Theresa if she was starting a new business. No. I finally just came out with the "enterprise" concept. Theresa burst into tears. She didn't think she was ever going to find a man, so she'd gone to the sperm bank to get pregnant and after a year still had no baby. Upon discovering that she was infertile, she considered herself a failure. This belief had so consumed her life that the dog was acting out.

A year later I ran into her at a show. The dog was performing in the top rankings again, and Theresa seemed more at peace. That one thought was a mental epidemic that nearly destroyed her home. Even worse, it was taking the joy away from their shared passion of showing.

Substance Abuse

I'm not saying that animals can't have ADD, but generally if they're all over the map, it's because they are mentally tracking a person who's scattered. They also can be very aware when someone in the household is having troubled thoughts, whether it's due to drug use (even prescription-drug use), mental illness, or severe physical trauma. I remember asking a guy once if his dog had a head injury. "No," he replied, "but *I'm* recovering from one."

I knew a lovely, funny, full-of-life woman who committed suicide a couple of years ago. I couldn't help but be reminded of how her dog was concerned about her depression three years prior to the tragic event. Her thoughts became like "cement," he'd told me. At the time, the woman let me know that she'd recently changed her medication. Unfortunately, the new medication wasn't doing its job.

Animals who've been living with a drug user can even begin to have confused thought patterns. I've connected with many adopted dogs where someone in their previous household was an obvious drug user. There were always people coming and going, creating very sketchy circumstances surrounding the dogs' lives.

One case truly surprised me. It involved a very clean-cut, handsome guy who didn't know why his dog was so aggressive. The dog—half rottweiler and half German shepherd—would come inches from my face and bark his head off. I didn't make eye contact and continued with the communication. I'm rarely startled by dogs barking at me, as it's part of the job, but this one actually scared me. I had to work very hard to turn off the fear in my mind and body.

Apparently, barking was the dog's way of being friendly. The young guy and his partner had adopted him at a very early age. When I connected with the dog, I had a sense that he was emotionally and mentally protecting a human whose thought pattern looked to be that of a drug user. I assumed the substance abuse was in the dog's prior home.

Alas, I was wrong. The man himself was a recovering drug addict, and the dog felt he still needed to try to organize the chaos. When his human wasn't thinking clearly, the dog—being a pleaser type—felt compelled to take over, because he was aware of how low-functioning the guy had been. Even after the man started recovery, left his partner, and began to clean up his life, the dog still didn't relax. Training at that point was imperative, and it enhanced their connection because the guy was not only handling his own circumstances, but was also able to directly manage the dog.

Louise and Dusty

When I met Dusty, he was on the canine equivalent of death row. He had bitten three people and was court-ordered into confinement at the pound. His termination date was yet to be announced, pending the judge's decision.

His lawyer and his owner, Louise, found me in order to see why he had attacked this latest person and how he felt about his upcoming euthanasia. Louise had told me on the phone that he'd originally been her son's dog, but the son was now in jail.

Through the chaotic thought pattern and the overprotective feeling that Dusty exuded, I sensed that his person had definitely been a drug user. Louise confirmed this. While under the son's care, at some point Dusty had been hit by a car. He sustained damage to his left shoulder and neck. Every person who'd tried to catch him approached from the left side and he reacted. He wanted to live, in a way, but he also felt that since he'd been the caretaker of the son who was now gone, he had no purpose.

Once all of this was out on the table, all of us—chiropractor, dog trainer, and I—were able to get to work. Louise had x-rays done, which proved that there *was* an old chronic injury that he was protecting.

The dog being in "jail" perfectly mirrored his original person's situation. But now we had to prove that Dusty could be in a social setting in order to save his life. Obviously, Dusty was more than just a dog to Louise: He was a reflection of saving the son whom she hadn't been able to help.

The first consultation I'd done with Dusty was over the phone. The next time it was in person. I had a court order to go to "death row" and work with him. (Very few people are allowed back there.) Because he was so unhappy with his prison sentence, he would go at the gate like he was out for blood. He seemed for all intents and purposes like a mass murderer when anyone approached his cell. His violent behavior confirmed for the staff that he was a killer, so the endless negative thought processes were just compounded. Underneath it all, I knew that he was a sweet, misguided dog who was mentally confused from being with a drug user, and that the physical trauma from this period of time remained in his body.

I sat next to his gate and mentally ran energy through his whole system, cleared his chakras, and sent in a Scalar Wave—a form of energy work that I do—to calm him down before I approached him with bodywork, mostly TTouch and acupressure. I had to leave every preconceived thought at the door and absolutely work for the highest good. Yes, it was scary. He was a big dog with ferocious teeth, and he had deep-seated beliefs about humans.

The first few times I did bodywork, Louise would muzzle him, but eventually we didn't even do that. The chiropractor visited a couple of times, and the dog trainer worked with him as well.

When the court date came up, we won Dusty's case. I say "we" because we all worked very hard for this dog. A year ago I got a thank-you note from Louise saying that it had been the three-year anniversary of Dusty's new life, and that he even had found a new best friend in a little boy down the street. More recently, I heard from Louise again to say that her son was out of jail and was clean from drugs. He and Dusty are as happy as can be now.

Dusty on death row in Colorado.

Mirror, Mirror on the Wall

Mirroring is so common that it has become the norm at this point in my work. I can't tell you how many times a week I'll be doing a phone session and will say something about the client's horse having a right-shoulder issue and the person will respond, "*I* have a rotator-cuff problem!" By protecting her own right shoulder, the rider may have created a problem in that area for the horse. But whether the person caused the situation, the two beings were matched up with preexisting shoulder problems, or there was an emotional component to the animal taking on its guardian's "stuff," no matter how you slice it, you then have a physiological reality that must be dealt with.

Many times I'll tell people that their animal companion has an adrenal issue, and the person will say, "Well, my own adrenals are shot." A woman on the phone the other day said that she'd had cancer on and off for 13 years and had lost a black Lab to the same form of the disease 9 years ago.

Mirroring isn't limited to illness, however; sometimes it applies to behavior as well. One woman called me about her dog being aggressive toward men. She had to put him in a crate if any male came to the door because he turned vicious. The dog told me that when he was young, there had been a man living there. The woman confirmed that she'd been married. Deep in her heart, she hadn't quite healed from her very bitter divorce. The dog was acting out *her* venom and spite at every opportunity.

Emerging Lessons

When a mirror is held up to your face because an animal is reflecting you back to yourself, you have the chance to take a deeper look and heal on a profound level. When mirrored behavior manifests in your animals, rather than being upset about it, use it as a jumping-off point. For example, perhaps it's not enough to get your cat on a homeopathic remedy; possibly *you* need to go on one as well.

Terri and K.C.

Terri called me because her horse K.C. wasn't doing that well. He was off his feed and seemed lethargic. When I checked in with him, his throat seemed full. Terri said that she was struggling with her thyroid and that her own throat seemed congested. Terri got K.C. when she was very young, and they were deeply connected. Since there were other physical issues with the horse, and he was up there in years, the obvious thing to do was to recommend that she have blood work run.

In the time remaining in the session, we took a deeper look at the throat aspect. In energetic terms, this area of the body corresponds to the fifth chakra, which is the place of expression in the world and to God. (In Part II, I'll go into the human and animal chakra systems in depth.) K.C. had been a magnificent show horse in his day. His form of expression had slowly run its course on some levels, although he was the elder of his barn.

I knew that Terri was very capable of doing energy work. Since there was a connection between the two of them in that they both had full throats, I told her about automatic writing and suggested that she vent all the things she wasn't saying. The technique is a great way to connect with your subconscious or your helpers (that is, your angels, spirit guides, and Higher Self). You simply close your eyes and let the pen go to work (of course, sometimes you start writing off the page and have to sneak a peak!). Eventually this can be an eyes-open exercise.

When Terri got off the phone, she started her automatic writing. What came up for her was fascinating: She discovered that she was upset because some of her friends had appeared to drop off the face of the earth. In addition, a deep fear about her own health was revealed. That very day her long-lost pals called her! She eventually addressed her own health issues, along with those of her horse.

Marianne and Hannah

Marianne and her dog Hannah spent years teaching me new lessons, even though I was just the hired gun. (Hannah was the other dog in the household of Marianne and Sparky, whose story you read about earlier.) Hannah mirrored her guardian's health and well-being, and she became the leader of this pack. When Marianne and her husband, Larry, got caught up in the stuff of life, Hannah marched them right out of it time and time again.

Hannah had an immune deficiency as well as Rocky Mountain spotted fever, which was a constant reminder to the family to stay on top of her—and their—immune system (which should be a great mirror for the whole world). Years ago Hannah wasn't coming out of an illness; actually, it was more like malaise. Marianne and Larry were also bogged down mentally, physically, emotionally, and professionally. One time when I checked in with Hannah, I had a sense that a vent in the house was suppressing her energy.

Marianne had the filters checked and, as you might guess, there was mold in them, which created a very toxic physical environment. Additionally, the mold and the oppressive atmosphere was a perfect metaphor for the other energies that were in the canyon where they lived. Apparently there was a Native American burial ground there. As much as they loved their house, this revelation about the mold was like an alarm system going off—it was time to move. They had the filters cleaned and the property cleared of any sort of spirits. They'd been responsible about the land, but they moved on. Everyone's health improved, with Hannah taking the lead.

Kelly and Ben

I have a friend named Kelly—a wonderful healer—
who had a dog who crossed over before I knew her. While
Kelly was finishing acupuncture school, her mother was
diagnosed with cancer and passed away. Around that
time, her father had gotten sick and subsequently died,
too. On top of everything, Kelly had a boyfriend who
wasn't emotionally safe for her. He had betrayed her continually, although she didn't know this until much later.
Kelly's foundation was being swept away from underneath her, and her trust was diminishing. Her dog, Ben,
was so aggressive that she couldn't even walk him safely
in the neighborhood. To her, however, he was the sweet-
est dog in the world . . . a safe harbor in a storm.

Kelly tried everything to fix the problem with Ben.
She finally gave in to the idea that she had her own "private" dog. She's a very gentle soul herself and as kind
and loving as could be. Here was this dog that *for her*
was the same. Ben guarded her from the world at times
when she didn't even know that she needed protection.
Therefore, she could travel her path peacefully as all her
losses continued to heal.

The next time that you see a dog that you think is
mean and nasty, remember that it may very well be somebody else's guardian angel!

Guardian Animals

It's amazing how many angels appear in the form of
our pets. They come for a short while and then depart
into the ether as we finally gain our footing, health, or

purpose. Frequently, an animal will stay on planet Earth for a very short while. It will come in, be an instant source of love, be stricken by a weird illness or have an accident, and out it goes. More often than not, this is so that *you* can be more fully alive. You can learn from animals to make different choices to honor your spirit.

Tia and Fyodor

A woman named Tia called me for a phone session a few years back. Her cat, Fyodor, was very lethargic, and after every possible form of blood work and testing, nothing had come up to indicate that anything specific was wrong.

Tia didn't at first tell me any of this. When I tuned in to the cat, I described him to the woman as otherworldly, with fabulous big eyes that watched over her when she slept. I told her that the cat loved to gaze at her face constantly. I then proceeded to let her know Fyodor's feelings, which organs seemed distressed, and what remedies should somewhat lessen the lethargy.

On the other end of the phone, Tia said that she had all the same symptoms herself. She'd been a doctor in Russia but couldn't take the medical boards here in the U.S. Instead, she was working as a dental assistant and putting herself through acupuncture school. Slowly but surely, her body was deteriorating from what seemed to be an autoimmune disorder that hadn't been diagnosed. (Knowing what I do now, I believe that it was probably a heavy-metal overload from working in a dentist's office.) She said that sometimes she was so tired that she couldn't make it to the couch. She would walk into her apartment and just lie down on the floor. The cat would come and rest next to her, and he'd just stare at her with his big green saucer eyes until she revived and got the energy to at least make dinner.

Months later the cat crossed over and an autopsy was performed. No results were found that conclusively revealed what sort of an illness he'd had or the cause of his death. The reason for his malaise was still a mystery.

I always had the sense that in no way was he a cat—I absolutely believe that he was an angel sent to heal her. Tia did get her energy back and continued with school. It's my hope that she's now out there practicing acupuncture with that angel watching over her work.

❖ *Chapter Five* ❖

FAMILY DYNAMICS

No matter how much cats fight, there
always seems to be plenty of kittens.
— Abraham Lincoln

We're asking a lot of our animal companions when
we expect them to be part of this cosmic madness,
and that includes multispecies living arrangements. We
plant other animals side by side with us in bed as we
sleep, forgetting about the direct competition they're in.
Then we compound that concept by expecting animals
to navigate elaborate areas (our homes), but with very
limited space to roam (our yards, if we have one). They
don't have dirt and dried pine needles under their paws
anymore. Instead they pitter-patter—or tear around—
over Persian rugs, exotic hardwoods, and Formica. And
we clean those surfaces with substances that are highly
toxic. Instead of listening to the wind changing, they
hear reruns of *Sex and the City* or rap music as background
noise. The scents in the household are all wrong, too—
they throw animals' electromagnetic fields into a frenzy.

Then we're breeding generations of over-vaccinated pets who eat commercial garbage. We're overtaxing these sensitive little creatures who not long ago were entirely dependent on their own senses and natural foods to survive.

Much of this (the Persian rugs versus the pine-needle bed, for example) is fine for a lot of them; in fact, it's desirable and sometimes even required. I understand that 10 to 20 generations down the line, golden retrievers will probably begin to think that a five-bedroom suburban home is the natural landscape, just as pigeons now look like—and for safety can blend in with—pavement, squirrels probably see telephone wires as a "natural" way to get around, and a deer might perceive a car as just another predator.

But a golden retriever in a five-bedroom home still *needs* a good romp, discipline in this newly modeled pack, and a few more old-school dog activities; otherwise, you could face a challenge.

Already it's stretching these animals' hardwired natures to ask them to accept us as "top dog" or benevolent herd leader. We've upped the ante and said, "That cat doesn't care that you're a rottie, but while I'm at work, you'll be taking the lead with her." Then we're shocked when this same dog drags us down the street on the leash. The house next door may have four cats and a dog bowing down to a screeching bird. . . . I've seen it all.

"Family dynamics" has taken on a whole new meaning. For whatever reason, many households get a puppy while they still have a couple of children in diapers. The mother ends up cleaning the poop of so many beings, but the one she resents is the dog. The puppy starts acting out all over the place, and the woman is shocked. She thinks that it must be learning disabled.

The other scenario I've seen a lot is what I call the "empty-nest-let's-get-a-horse" syndrome. It goes like this: The woman rode in her youth and may even have been an expert rider. That last kid goes off to college, and Mom thinks that she wants a horse without any baggage, so she gets a yearling whom she'll train. Something goes askew, which may or may not include a broken bone, and now "baggage" has been created with this yearling. The part that people forget when they want a horse is that it's still a 1,200-pound baby!

Knowing Your Pets' History

Where did your animal companions come from? There are some experts who believe that once a feral cat, always a feral cat. Even the kitten of such an animal will have lived with the fear of humans and will instinctively bolt from unfamiliar sounds because those sensations were experienced while it was in the womb, making it not the best choice if you're looking for a lap cat.

Often people aren't conscious of what their animal was bred for. Did they end up with a herding dog? Are they expecting it to sit quietly with someone who's watching TV or doing homework after being in a crate all day? If you can take a look at some of the specific qualities of the breed, at the very least you have a chance to create fun games that allow the natural instincts of your animal companion to be fully expressed.

At dinnertime, my dog, Olivia, wants to herd the cat, who immediately gets on her hind legs and prepares to kung fu fight her. Olivia runs off, and their instincts create a game. They chase each other through the house, taking turns in the lead. Was I cautious when this play began? Absolutely. But now it has evolved into a wildly entertaining ritual three or four times a day that either one can start with just the flick of an ear.

The labyrinth of coexistence has a natural order. We're not sleeping in a fern bed with a canopy of leaves and branches above us, hearing birdcalls throughout our dreams. Still, even though we're no longer entwined in nature's web, those same sensations of being part of the bigger picture can be established in our human-made abodes.

Animals are stellar at setting up a natural order— a code of honor and boundaries—in a flock, a herd, a pack, or a pride. But now that we're mixing species, many, many households end up in a free-for-all.

It's All about Leadership

Even if one or more of your animals is the manager of the house (or even the neighborhood), you're still the leader. Dogs and cats that have even a slight amount of nervousness or anxiety shouldn't be in charge of a household—it's too much for them. However, there *are* some with personalities that can handle that and more.

If you have two manager types—a cat and a dog, say—and they're competing for jobs, put one in charge of the front yard and the other in charge of the back. Then *you* run the house. Or the cat can manage the inside of the house, while the dog watches the outside. Or the kitchen could be run by the cat, and the dog might oversee the living room.

Be mindful of triggers for your animal companions, particularly food and your time and attention (not to mention possession of toys or living space). Setting everyone up in a win-win-win (a win for each animal *and* the overall harmony of the household) is best. Even if it takes a little extra effort, separating pets around feeding may be necessary. Giving them each private playtime with you could also be important, and finding ways for them to enjoy *one another* would be ideal.

Even though my dog and cat can be competitive about who's the best in the house, there are moments between them that are so sweet and kind. At those times, it's as if the feelings of—dare I say it?—love (that may be a bit much . . . how about *caring?*) emanate in the space between them. My two horses are the same way. Watching those dynamics at work can be entertaining, enlightening, and endearing.

Ann, Iris, and Buddy

Ann called because she was having trouble with Iris and Buddy, two dogs who weren't especially fond of each other. It had gotten to the point that Buddy began urinating in the house, so then Iris started following suit.

Originally the family had consisted of Ann, Mariah (the oldest dog), and Iris. While Iris and Mariah had their squabbles, they followed a natural order. Then Ann acquired Buddy after a friend died. Iris and Mariah ganged up a bit on the newcomer. So what did Ann do? She felt sorry for Buddy. And what did *he* do? He became incorrigible.

Sadly, he and Ann were also grieving over the shared loss of Buddy's former human. As a result, he got special attention from Ann, which also corresponded with his acting out. This fact just added to Iris and Mariah's feeling that he was a freeloader. Then Mariah crossed over, and Iris and Buddy didn't create a new natural order between them. It was a free-for-all as to who was going to be in charge.

Ann frequently came home from work distracted by life (just as we all do). Both Iris and Buddy would see this as an opportunity to try to take control of the household, as the pictures they got from Ann were all over the map. Even her posture indicated someone on overload. Rather than correct Buddy, she always scolded Iris, who was more likely to still accept Ann as the leader. But because she never established that sort of relationship with Buddy, he didn't show her respect and could still act like a puppy at age seven. Iris just thought Buddy was impossible.

This is a very common setup. As much as the psychic part was important in establishing the feelings that Ann, Iris, and Buddy each had, the crux of our session became about reframing perceptions and helping Ann gain control of the household.

It's unfair of us as humans, the more evolved species, not to step in as the managing partners. If we don't, the living situation can become one of confusion, even mayhem.

Terri and K.C. (Revisited)

Terri, the woman who explored automatic writing in the story from the last chapter, called me on another occasion about her horse K.C. He was supposed to be her up-and-coming star in the show ring, but he was acting out all over the place. He was naughty! He bucked and wouldn't move forward when cued to, in addition to further antics. Not only was he mischievous, but people were starting to question whether he had a screw loose or even harbored evil intent. Deep down in her heart, Terri knew that neither was true, but when faced with such behavior, she started to question her judgment. And after enough bad incidents, fear set in.

When we arranged for the phone session, all I had was the picture of the horse from an e-mail, and I'd forgotten to ask Terri about the other animals in her household and at the barn. But K.C. was quick to tell me about the scenario at home.

K.C. had good breeding and was expected to be a big winner. He told me in no uncertain terms just how gorgeous he was! He let me know that he didn't like working in the arena at home (the location of his serious disobedience) because he was being watched by Terri's old retired superstar, who let him know that in no way, shape, or form, would or could K.C. ever be the horse that he had been. In addition, another mare there required a lot of attention from Terri.

Terri was quite amused but not at all surprised that her retired superstar would behave like that. He had been number one and had won everything, and he was still handsome and regal. So K.C. was suffering a bit from the elder's chiding and had low self-esteem, even though he claimed to know he was gorgeous!

K.C. didn't need the pressure from the other horse, so I suggested that he not be ridden at home until he had already shown—and furthermore, could prove to himself—that he was the superstar he was bred to be. I asked Terri if there was a public arena she could haul a trailer to or ride to, or if she might take lessons at the trainer's barn for a while to straighten out K.C.'s behavior. She said yes, she could go to the trainer.

We also talked about building K.C.'s self-esteem. Because he was so smart, I suggested not laboring on anything too long. When the horse got a lesson, it was time to move on. I said to let him know how brilliant he was and then teach him something else and allow him to perfect it. He needed to experience success. And by doing short lessons and not being given the opportunity to misbehave, he did.

Terri started riding K.C. at the trainer's barn with excellent results. Not only did he do well there, he went on to win at the first show he was entered in. Since then, he has built up his pride, can withstand the knocks from the elder superstar, and has become a star in his own right.

Terri had to first see beyond her conception of K.C. as being a problem child and understand what was really bothering him. She made simple adjustments, and in no time the whole situation was transformed.

The Hierarchy of Roles

Every home I walk into for a session is like watching a Tony Award–winning play or reading a Pulitzer Prize–winning novel. Who is the hero? Who or what is preventing that protagonist from reaching his or her full potential? How does each character's potential get recognized? What is the tragic flaw of the leader of the pack, pride, herd, or flock? Who started the mutiny? Who is the takeover artist?

In my house, the latter role belongs to the dog, Olivia. The cat, Alexandria, and I lived by ourselves for years. I'll still try to feed and address her first, but Olivia barges right in on the greeting and wants to help make dinner. We all know the sound of a happy tail hitting the floor with heavenly conviction. Olivia is so Scorpio (that is, competitive) that if Alexandria is in trouble, you can really hear that tail thump! She actually smiles if the cat is being scolded.

Once I was called to a woman's house because her kitten was pooping in the hallway. He was very cute, and the woman absolutely adored him. I asked him why he was going to the bathroom in the hallway, and he let me know in no uncertain terms that the older cat had told him that this was the way to get attention in that house!

I know a gal who has a barn full of warmblood horses. (Originally bred in Europe, a "warmblood" is a combination of a hot- and a cold-blooded horse.) They all carry the potential to compete at a very high level. Two of the female horses would spit nails at each other if they could—Tonya Harding, look out . . . these two would take each other out of any race! One of the horses was imported from Germany; the other was bred here in the States. Both were queens, so my suggestion was to make one the queen of hearts and the other that of diamonds.

Jealousy isn't the only sentiment that plays out among animals. Sometimes admiration is so huge that one pet loses its identity in another. Let's say that you have a number two dog who's perfectly suited for that secondary position—it has allowed the number one dog to make all the decisions. Then when number one dies, number two is at a loss because it was completely defined by the other dog. This comes up a couple of times a month in the course of my sessions.

At that point, you have to be the guide until the number two dog starts thinking for itself. Once some of the grieving has been processed and the deceased has been fully honored, it's not a bad idea to get another animal. That number two dog may have a karmic need to stay locked in the same role, or it might take this opportunity to come into its own.

Every herd, pack, pride, and flock has positioning. It's important to be aware if your dog or cat is a type A personality before you introduce another such animal. If you're going to bring in two alpha bitches, be prepared for how you might distract them or create more harmony when things are tense.

Betsy and Maxwell

A woman named Betsy called me because her husband had a top-winning German shepherd, Maxwell, whom he was retiring from Schutzhund trials and bringing into the home. Schutzhund is a three-part competition that's based on tracking, obedience, and protection. The last element can seem rather menacing to the average person. Betsy was a bit intimidated by this great master of the discipline and was unsure how to manage with the dog now in the household.

I spent a lot of time with Maxwell and his people talking about his devotion, loyalty, and self-command. We appealed to his sense of pride in now taking on this new job of being a dog in the home. We established that

Betsy was above him in the pack. By the end of the session, she felt quite confident. I also suggested that she and her husband have a retirement party for the dog.

I got a very nice e-mail that things were going well: The relationship between Maxwell and Betsy was progressing nicely. About a year later, the husband realized that he missed the connection with a dog while they were building a team as well as the excitement of competition, so he got another German shepherd. But retiring one show dog and then having another enter the household can be tricky, especially if you have two unneutered males with big egos and lots of pride.

We did a session on managing the retired champion who'd done it all and the newbie thinking that he *could* do it all without training. This is always a challenge. It can be done, but there definitely needs to be serious ground rules and lots of patience. Again, Betsy became an excellent manager of these two dogs.

She didn't want to knock down the ego of the new dog too much, as this attitude is actually what makes for a winning spirit. Yet she had to maintain a fragile balance so that the elder was honored, especially since he had gone from superior show dog in an aggressive sport to a loving household pet.

The New Kid on the Block

At some point, most of us have had drama in the dynamics of the household when we've added a new dog, cat, spouse, or baby. (For some cats, even adding furniture can send them under the bed because it spells *change!*)

Often, particularly with cats, a new kitten will enter a household and demand a lot of everyone, even a 17-

year-old cat who wants no part of someone new. Believe it or not, asking a kitten or puppy to play gently will have an effect, whether it's with you or with another animal. Find ways to play with a new puppy or kitten so that it's not pouncing on an elder animal.

A very common dynamic that can upset the hierarchy is to bring just one more cat into a household that's full of them. The cats have already established who they are and what each of them does. So you can imagine what happens next: The one who's "pissed off" takes it upon him- or herself to act out . . . literally. Then as the house begins to stink, more join in the cat games—kitty see, kitty do.

The challenge in this type of situation is partly one of management. This happened to someone I recently had a consultation with, and I reminded her that she had to take back her house. It was time for a powwow, and she needed to reclaim her power. I'd been called in to deal with the cat problem, but of course this was a metaphor for other aspects of the woman's life. She wanted to believe that the house was theirs, too. No question, it *was* their home, but were they paying the mortgage? No. *She* was the boss.

Think of the cats like kids: Would you let a five-year-old determine what goes on in the household? How fair would that be to him or her? And why would you give your authority away? If you surrender it to your own *cats,* where else is there a power leak? This creates way too much stress for everyone. There are times when you have to step in and take the reins.

James and Abe

A friend of mine, James, told me that when his fiancée moved in, things were going pretty well with his Jack Russell terrier, Abe, who loved his bride-to-be. However, Abe and James had lived together—just the two of them—for nearly eight years, and although the dog *seemed* to take to the new addition swimmingly, one day there was a poop next to the door. Days later when James was in the bathroom shaving, he looked in the mirror at Abe. She quite boldly stared back and then peed on the rug.

James was outraged. He turned around and glared at her, saying, "This is *my* house. You will not misbehave." James inquired if I thought that she got it. I asked if she'd peed again. He said no. I told him that she got it.

James mentioned to me that he was worried about how the dog would take it when he and his fiancée got married and had a baby. I reminded him that Abe had been an extraordinary full-time manager, and an infant wasn't going to take away from her life; rather, it would add to the task list that her type A personality balanced. Abe would love having more obligations.

Many, many animals thrive on responsibility, even if it's our ingrained belief that particular large-breed dogs are dangerous in some settings. If you can release that picture and give them a job, your anxiety—and theirs—could instantly be quelled.

People don't believe how much power their speech can carry. Not only do animals understand many words, they certainly know the intention underlying them. If you're backing away from your words—for example, saying "Sit" as a question and not a command or speaking it gently—you can bet the dog is picking up on your timidity or insecurity. If you say "Sit" three times before the dog obeys, you've obviously trained it that you have to repeat yourself before it will finally listen. Even if you've given over some of the managerial positions in the household to your pets, speaking with authority aids in the overall harmony.

A woman called me about her golden retriever who suffered from allergies. She suspected that there was an emotional component. She'd lost her other dog to cancer six months prior, and the loss saddened the entire household, including the woman, her husband, her three-year-old daughter, and the golden. So they added a puppy to the mix. The golden retriever loved the new dog, but the woman found the puppy very difficult to train. The older animal could sense that for both adults the grief was triggering deeper feelings. For the woman, it related to her abandonment by her own mother; for the husband, it brought up issues with his father.

Neither had resolved these inner conflicts from their upbringing, yet they were trying to make theirs the perfect home. Their own grief and guilt was driving them, and the road became bumpy with the loss of the other dog. That dynamic was keeping the golden retriever and the puppy in an adrenal overload—thus, the ongoing battle with allergies for the golden and the unwanted behavior from the puppy.

Bringing Up Baby

A couple was having their first child. They had two cats who'd been the "babies" of the house up until that point, and they were nervous about how the cats were going to take the introduction of a new creature. I said, (1) quit worrying, and (2) employ them.

I talked about all the babysitting that the cats could do. They could also be in charge a little more around the house. That way, while the couple was adjusting to the new hours, they could rest assured that the cats had the bugs under control or would watch the driveway.

Years ago, a client called saying that she was pregnant and that her dog had just bitten the furnace man. She was terrified about what the dog would be like with the new baby. The dog had felt as if the house was being threatened when this guy walked in to fix something without the woman being home. The dog let me know that he was already aware of the pregnancy, sensing his guardian's new vulnerability. In fact, he was taking the watchdog role *way* too seriously.

We also found out about his low self-esteem. He felt that he wasn't doing enough, so I suggested to the woman that she bring in a trainer to help. The dog had to understand that he wasn't in full command of the household, yet at the same time, he needed to know that he was doing enough even if he just lay next to the woman while she was reading on the couch.

We also agreed that he would be "off duty" when she was at home to remind him that the human had it handled. In addition, we showed him that the woman was in charge with subtle training methods. We converted her fear into something more productive, creating jobs for the dog throughout the pregnancy until the baby arrived. Consequently, he was relaxed when the little one came and was a wonderful helper. The woman sent me a great picture of dog and baby.

Great Dynamics

Acknowledging who and what the animals are can also aid in the family dynamics. Multispecies living requires certain adjustments on our part in order to understand our pets' very basic needs. Sometimes when a dog is anxious, for example, it's simply a case of finding a way to make it feel safe, while at the same time giving it a purpose.

Julia, Sierra, and Snoosh

Great dynamics sometimes literally can be life-saving. Sierra was a 12-year-old girl who was helping her mother, Julia, feed horses at the barn. While Sierra was off in a feed room, the family dog, Snoosh, rushed in and grabbed her. Sierra thought she was being attacked at first, which would have been so unlike Snoosh, her lifelong babysitter. Snoosh dragged her to the barn aisle, where Julia was lying facedown. The little girl found a phone, called 911, and helped the emergency workers when they airlifted her unconscious mother to Seattle.

Julia didn't remember anything about the accident and Sierra didn't see it, so I asked the horse and Snoosh what had happened. Apparently, Julia had leaned into the stall to pick something up and had startled the horse.

According to the horse, it was his front foot that struck Julia and broke her jaw.

After a few weeks in the hospital, Julia came home, but the dog was depressed. When we checked in with Snoosh, we discovered that she was still worried about the concussion and didn't think she'd reacted in time. Julia had a big talk with Snoosh, letting her know that she was the big dog hero just as Sierra was the big kid hero. After that, Snoosh started acting like herself again.

That's a good example of dynamics at their best: As a result, Julia's life was probably saved. And back at home, one simple acknowledging conversation between Julia and Snoosh lifted the dog's spirits. Snoosh definitely was aware of who she was in the household and what she'd needed to do to get help.

Amy and Poggio

My mother and I were having lunch with her friend Jemmi in the summer of 2004. Jemmi got a call from her daughter Amy in England, who told her that she'd made the Olympic team for three-day eventing but hadn't decided which of the two horses she competed on would be going to Athens with her. It was between Poggio and another.

On the one hand, the other horse was bred for this sort of thing: An elegant warmblood, he was sponsored by a private owner and was as cool as a cucumber in the face of such stress. Poggio, on the other hand, was a thoroughbred who rose from rags to riches. Thoroughbreds aren't generally thought of as Olympic bound—they're usually regarded strictly as racehorses.

When Jemmi got off the phone, I could sense the struggle. I'd talked to Poggio years before and knew that he was a true partner for Amy. He'd been picked up for under $5,000, while the other horse had had a giant price tag and possessed the breeding to handle Olympic-level competition. However, Poggio put his all into every event; and any shortcomings were made up for by his gallant, heartfelt efforts. I knew that if the other horse were picked, Poggio would, given the opportunity, hurl himself off a cliff.

Thankfully, Poggio, the underdog, outdid himself and won a place on the team, becoming the Seabiscuit of the Athens Olympics. Amy and Poggio won a bronze medal, thus proving just how strong their winning dynamic could be under the most intense pressure.

❖ *Chapter Six* ❖

> # SETTING THE TONE

*Of all God's creatures there is only one
that cannot be made the slave of the leash. That one is the cat. If
man could be crossed with a cat it would improve man, but
it would deteriorate the cat.*
— Mark Twain

Recently my dog, Olivia, and I took an agility class. I knew that Olivia would have great skills in this area, and I only hoped that as her leader, *I* could be as good! During the introduction to the class, the teacher actually told us to always keep a smile on our faces and to never get after the dogs with a harsh tone of voice.

I thought, *Of course we're going to smile—this is fun.* In no time, though, I saw why she had to give us this reminder. We humans wanted to get everything right so badly that our frustration and emotions went up, and our understanding and intelligence went down. In that case, what's the payoff for the animals? Why *should* they perform for us?

When the humans in the class were excited, the dogs shot through the various tubes, poles, and hoops with very little instruction. It was as if they'd been home watching a "How to Do Agility" video while we were at work! If we set the tone with enthusiasm, they were happy to go along with us, entertain us, and be team players. It wasn't the extra-special treats I bought for the occasion that inspired Olivia; it was being part of that fun activity with me.

Of course that seems like a lesson in: "Hey, Joan, be aware of the obvious!" But how many times do we drop the keys when we're in a hurry, and while we fumble for them, the cat shoots out of the door? Frustration then keeps us at arm's length as she has a field day running just a few steps ahead, apparently knowing that we're late. Or consider if you have a follow-up call with the human-resources department for a fantastic new job. You're nervous, and that's the day the bird sits and screams as if your home is a torture chamber. The animals aren't trying to sabotage us . . . they're simply picking up on our moods.

Our horses (usually) graciously accept us as the leader. Then at the show, when we get distracted by a competitor's new animal, we're surprised when ours suddenly isn't partnering up with us in the ring. Or we get preoccupied with barn gossip, and the wheelbarrow we pass every day somehow surprises our horse and it spooks. The animals aren't the ones who are distracted—frequently *we* are.

Whether its original genetic predisposition is to be predator or prey, every life-form is out for safety and survival. In our modern overstimulated society, most of us don't struggle for those basics of food, water, and shelter anymore—we're perfecting *comfort*. We do seek approval and control, but all of us varied species have a new set of things that can trigger the "fight, flight, or fright" behavior: Our emotional response to a spouse, to a child, or even to our animal companions can elicit those reactions. We respond in the same way we would have if we were still in a hunter-gatherer world and the last berry patch was frozen, leaving us no food for the winter.

Harmony

Claiming your power within yourself isn't about control, but rather is about having some command over how you want to respond to events and then how you want your animals to respond to you. Coming home from work and being available is a good start. Harmony in the household will not only benefit your animal companion . . . it will also reverberate in all aspects of your life. Setting the tone of harmony is a must, even when faced with what appears to be just the opposite.

For example, I love to set the tone before I ride. This is especially true with my horse Rollie, who can enter an arena like Kramer in a *Seinfeld* episode, with his hair and feet going the opposite direction from me. We're attached simply by the reins. (You can almost hear Kramer saying, "I'm all hopped up on Cinnamon Twirls.") I know Rollie could fling me to Nova Scotia with a mere buck. Being annoyed and saying to him, "Dude, chill" won't save my life in the saddle. However, slowly putting my gloves on, adjusting the stirrups, and climbing on the mounting block all the while telling him how heroic he is and how we get to glide around like Fred and Ginger changes his state. Letting him know how thankful I am that we get to learn together enhances the whole tone and quality of the ride.

Recently, I went to a barn where the trainers, Jen and Tammy, had gotten two terriers since I'd been there last. After having sessions with many of the horses in training, they wanted me to talk to their dogs. These two were so assertive. (Sometimes I think that *terrier* in some other language means "too smart for its own good"!) They were incredibly astute about the regular activities around this very busy barn and knew what every other animal on the farm *should* be up to. This overachieving terrier authority included, but was not limited to, what the cats were doing. And in the dogs' humble opinions, the cats were *doing* nothing. These dogs thought of themselves as better hunters, which led to another problem: The dogs were chasing the barn cats, and since terriers have such a "kill" instinct, this scared both Jen and Tammy.

Jen had been given a kitten, the kind she'd been waiting for her entire life, and the trainers named him "Puppy Cat." Brilliant. The dogs had terrified the other cats, but they found Puppy Cat to be exactly that—somehow the tone was set, and to them this kitty was, in fact, a puppy (cat). Puppy Cat saw himself as more of a dog, too, and it worked out perfectly for all.

Be Careful What You Think

As simplistic as it sounds, part of your role as an animal communicator is tracking your own thoughts, just as your dog or cat would!

I met a woman and her dog, a courageous German shepherd who had a degenerative spine disease. He had loved the full expression of his body, so this condition was very difficult for him. All of the woman's friends had been telling her to put him out of his misery. She felt beaten down by their opinions and was torn about what to do. Not ready to surrender and follow the advice of her friends, she consulted with me to ask her dog if he wanted to try wheels or if he was ready to give up. He told me that he wanted to try the wheels, even though he didn't think that they'd work.

We had another session a couple of months later. The woman had parked her car in front of my house, but when I looked out the window, I couldn't see animal or owner. The next thing I knew, along came this dog racing full speed ahead, his front legs reaching out like a greyhound, with wheels in the rear. The woman was way behind in the dust!

They're just hanging on to that animal is a thought that invades many brains. But how do you know that the animal isn't hanging on to *them?* How can you be sure that the family isn't getting the most fantastic lesson about the dignity of death? Death is the process of entering that other world. Why would you allow your judgment to stop someone from truly facilitating an expert journey?

The Power of Labels

Labeling a condition—whether it's age, an illness, an emotion, a behavior, or circumstances—establishes a tone and also sets actions into motion as though they were following a preformed track. Just a small shift in tone can lift the spirits of an aging, misbehaving, or health-challenged animal companion faster than it can with most human adults.

Age is a particularly great example. Energetically, my horse Gabrielle is six or seven, but chronologically I can tell you that her hooves have been planted on the ground longer than that. I have to do a lot of math to remember how many years I've had my cat, Alexandria, in order to remember her age on planet Earth.

A new horse came into a barn where I was boarding my animals. He was an elderly guy, almost literally a bag of bones—and arthritic and tired ones at that. However, the horse had very kind, grateful eyes. Everyone who walked up to his stall said, "Poor guy"—and he did look pretty broken. I suggested that we call him the "wise one." In no time, his whole demeanor changed. His eyes perked up and he started gaining weight.

A trainer friend of mine reserved the center of her barn for the senior-citizen horses. I suggested that she call it the Wisdom Center! When we change our thoughts and then our words, suddenly we can transform the surrounding spirit. The animal's actual age may have nothing to do with how it's feeling or what it wants to do. Honor the spirit, not the number.

Is our tendency to judge others for hanging on to their older animals really about our own fear of aging? This culture idolizes youth. We put people away who are past a certain age. We can't bear to look at them. As animals grow old, we have an opportunity to learn about this process. It happens to them before our very eyes much sooner than it does us.

Like many people, some animals don't want to get old. They opt out at the first exit sign. Others truly bless us with grace. Joy comes in all forms. Even if your dog was once the fastest dog on the block, it may get great pleasure from lying on the couch with you now. Other dogs may have a very difficult time after enjoying a lifetime of great physical activity. Some horses may love being out in the pasture after years of showing; others really don't. One cat may live daily just to sleep with you. Others wouldn't want to be alive if they couldn't dangle from the curtains. Our perspective on joy and what fulfills us shifts along with our lifestyles. We must honor the same in our animals.

I once went to the home of a couple who had three dogs. The oldest one could barely get off the floor to greet me. The other two nearly knocked me over as I walked in the door. We could look at that elder and easily think, *It's time for her to go.* But that dog was very content. Her best energy was in the morning; she loved the frenzy as the people got ready for work. She saw her old self in the precocious puppy. After the humans had gone, she was happy to sleep until the evening. Again, the dinnertime rush filled her with joy. She didn't want anyone feeling sorry for her—she just needed a little push out the door to go to the bathroom twice a day.

Projecting the Positive

Being diagnosed with an illness is another time when we shrink-wrap ourselves into a package of doom and gloom and enfold our animals in it with us. This affects us even more if we've experienced the deaths of other animals (or humans) from that particular illness. We plunk that tragedy right onto our own experience.

I recently read a report about how Washington University in St. Louis has conducted studies on the brain with regard to projecting into the future. Interestingly enough, MRIs showed that there was activity in three parts of the brain whether someone was daydreaming about the future or remembering the past. In other words, our memory is part of projecting into the future—it's natural for us to go there. The trick with effecting a change and setting the tone you want is to be aware of the thoughts that are attached to the diagnosis and being vigilant about envisioning a new outcome.

The word *cancer* can invoke countless emotions, pictures, and thoughts. It's a dense, low-vibration word, meaning that it carries the weight of all that has happened with respect to cancer collectively. The term can take on a life of its own. We all have thoughts and feelings around it and have experienced loss because of it. We've all witnessed major unpleasant changes in other people's lives. Very few of us find the illness to be a blessing, so it's hard not to get caught up in the group consciousness around it all.

Suppose a cat is diagnosed with cancer. Humans think about what that could mean, usually in terms of the worst-case scenario. They latch onto the weight of what cancer has felt like for them or their deep-seated belief system about the disease, and then suddenly they're riding down a fast-moving escalator of hopelessness. The negativity alone could smother the cat—and all the while the beloved animal is also struggling with the cancer itself.

Frequently I ask clients to reframe that cancer picture and see it as simply naughty cells. Then we can either contain them or get the rest of the body so healthy that they aren't welcome there anymore. At that point there's a fighting chance for a different outcome. Of course, the will of the animal and whether it's the creature's time is also a question, and that's not up to us. However, if the will is there and you want to put up a fight, don't start from a downtrodden place.

A Final Journey

About a year before my mother died, I asked her what she wanted to do, and she said that she knew just the tour to go on! She wanted to visit central Europe—Poland, the Czech Republic, and Hungary. My mother loved traveling; my father hated it. I was the perfect escort, so I arranged to take a month off and go.

The week before we left, my mom underwent probably her harshest chemotherapy treatment to date. Up until that point, she actually had managed quite well, but this last round was more than a little challenging. Not only that, but the cancer had progressed and was taxing her entire system. Everyone we knew thought that I was insane to take her to Europe, because she couldn't walk from a restaurant to the car even if valet parkers delivered it right to the door.

My theory was different. I figured that *at the very least* we could skip all the tours that the travel company offered and just sit and have coffee in Prague. We could also do the same in Kraków, in Budapest, and in Warsaw. It would be something different from lying in her bed at home, and the transportation and accommodations would be taken care of. All we really had to do was get in an elevator. Worst-case scenario, we could order room service in our hotel.

I arranged for a wheelchair with the tour company just in case, but I never told them why. It was a company that catered to senior citizens, so a wheelchair wasn't an unreasonable request; I didn't have to say the word *cancer.*

We met in Warsaw. My mother looked exhausted but so happy that night in the hotel lobby. Every morning, I aligned myself and briefly did a little bit of energy work on her. I would send energy through her whole system, as if I were hitting the restart button for the day. After the first tour or activity, I would send her to her room for a two-hour nap, and I'd work out and meditate. Mind you, at home she would sleep all day. Then in the afternoon we would do something else. After that was dinner, and then there was walking on the cobblestone streets, more eating, and maybe a glass of wine—and certainly a dessert.

On that trip, nobody knew that she had cancer. Nobody got to place the weight of their perception of sickness on her or feel sorry for her. We never even saw the wheelchair. It wasn't a form of denial—it was making a choice. We chose joy. We looked like a mother and daughter having fun, and that's exactly what we were.

Through a little bit of energy work and lots of positive thought, we waltzed through central Europe. We ended up doing every tour and many more activities. (We even learned to polka!) Sometimes I didn't get her back to her room before midnight, and we'd have to be up very early the next day to get to a lecture about the history of whichever city we were in. We put the best picture forward to others, and *I* didn't accept anything less than that image either. As a result, we had the time of our lives.

Many of my clients have been successful by making these choices as well. Sometimes people aren't even aware they're making them—the health-challenged animal just seems to magically outlast the vet's prediction, and then everyone gets on board with the miracle.

Peggy and Shadow

Peggy had come to me with her dog Shadow, a golden retriever. At that time he was about 12 or 13 years old, and she wondered how he was doing. He expressed to me that there had been a number of life changes since they first came together. He told me that Peggy had overcome an illness (cancer, as it turned out), she'd gone through a very hard divorce, and they had moved. I could tell by his spirit and resilience that he was one of those guys who took everything in stride. They were a very good pair.

About a year later I received a frantic call from Peggy: Shadow had been diagnosed with nasal cancer. She'd done one round of chemo, and the Western-medicine vets had given Shadow only a couple of months to live. Even the holistic vet didn't hold much hope.

Shadow and Peggy came over. The dog was okay with his situation—he was just a little more tired than usual and on occasion the tumor pressed up against his eyes, giving him a headache—but he wasn't ready to die.

I did some energy work on Shadow and used my Rife machine (an instrument designed in the 1930s by Dr. Royal Rife as a cancer treatment using sound waves as high-frequency signals to rebalance the cells). In addition, Peggy and I talked about other things that can raise the frequency: being happy, finding fun, good food, and so on.

At least another year passed, and when I received a phone message from Peggy, I thought that Shadow must have passed and she wanted me to talk to a new dog. Boy, was I wrong! Shadow was doing great, but as a precaution Peggy wanted a second round of energy work. Another year passed. Eventually we did have the consultation about letting him go, and he finally crossed over. However, Peggy and Shadow got a couple of extra years to enjoy each other's company.

FREQUENCY EXPLAINED

Frequency is an important factor in energy or vibrational medicine—the higher, the better. For example, if you think of an unpleasant situation in your life, your whole aura and being can drag you down to a low place. If you concentrate on happier moments in your life, suddenly that focus can uplift your whole spirit. It's nice to be in charge of your own frequency, but it can also be affected by outside influences.

Things that negatively affect my frequency include:

- Pollution
- Clutter
- Electromagnetic fields
- Someone else's bad mood
- Family turmoil
- Preservatives in food
- Anything in excess
- Having to do a job I dislike
- Living in limbo (unless I'm in a state of expectancy that something fantastic will manifest)
- Jet lag
- The news

FREQUENCY EXPLAINED, CONT'D.

Things that raise my frequency are:

- Dancing with abandon
- Singing along to silly songs
- Museums, a great theatrical performance, and fabulous music
- Being at a beautiful natural location
- Organic foods
- Minerals and crystals
- Puppy breath
- A monkey trying to grab my earring
- Laughter
- Being in love
- Dinner with friends
- A great ride with either of my horses
- Having my cat chase a light
- Horses in a far field with their tails swaying in the breeze
- Pretending that my dog and I are preparing for the Frisbee Olympics
- Exercise
- The presence of my dog and cat at bedtime and upon waking
- A massage
- Pampering myself with bath salts or a nourishing lotion (as long as they don't contain parabens)
- Wind chimes
- A moment of success
- A really great daydream

Make your own lists. You may find many of these same things on them, along with others that are meaningful just to you.

The Power of Belief

If I've seen the power of belief once, I've seen it a hundred times. Seriously, so many animals (and people) will far outlive the "expiration dates" that vets (or doctors) give them. Now, if your animal's condition does decline, you can't blame yourself. It's simply the journey of that soul—it may have nothing to do with you. You can only support the animal's choice. Your agenda can be that it get better, but in the end, you can't rewrite its contract.

Life hasn't gone perfectly for many of us, so that place of hopelessness has our own devastation and familiarity imprinted on it. But we do have a choice there; we can think a different thought and be more buoyant about the situation and see how that uplifts us. Even if the relief is only momentary—how great is that?

One of the hardest times to set the tone is when we rescue an animal. Our heart has gone out to this other soul in an effort to be a safe harbor for it. The word *rescue* has a thousand implications, but they're rarely positive, appealing instead to that hurt little child in all of us who's longing to be saved. Equally, it can appeal to that unhealthy part in us that's trying to save everything. The collective consciousness around that word has the weight of a thousand-pound meteor. People will preface an introduction to a dog, cat, or horse with, "This is my 'rescue.'" That phrasing begs you to feel sorry for the animal or give it an excuse for a certain type of behavior.

The animal can remain shy and introverted or worse, incorrigible. So many people *allow* unbelievable behavior because it was rescued. It goes like this: *It was a rescue, poor thing. Nobody will care about it like I will. It deserves affection, and therefore if it ruins every Persian rug with pee and*

poops on my desk, it's okay because I love it—it's my rescue.
Then you're controlled by your thoughts and feelings
around the word *rescue.*

Dogs and even cats love boundaries just as all beings
do. We may press up against them—that's one way we
define who we are—but we do need them. If we just
drove on the freeway at whatever speed we wanted, there
would be mayhem. "Rescue" dogs need boundaries more
than anyone. Having rules of the pack creates safety for
them.

Whenever people introduce me to their dogs or cats
as I walk in the door, telling me that this animal is so-and-
so, that one is such and such, and this one over here is
"my rescue," I just comment, "That one over there is the
lucky one. The day you rescued him was the day you both
got lucky." I also say, "Look around your house. Does this
look like a rescue facility? No. Then how could this dog
possibly still be a rescue?"

My friend Paula called me to see if I'd do a session. I
told her no. She was stunned and asked, "Why not?"

I replied, "Because I know exactly why you're calling.
You think that Boo is depressed."

"She is, but how did you know?"

Of course I wanted to say, "Because I'm a pet psychic," but in truth I told her, "You got that dog, and she
was in shock and depressed. Then you had a baby who's
now five, and you're *still* treating Boo the same way, so
she thinks she's depressed—and then *you* get depressed.
You fulfill each other's prophecy. It's perfect."

"Oh," Paula said. She had to rethink how she treated
Boo. I told her to pretend that there was nothing wrong
and see what would happen. After a couple of weeks,
there *was* a huge change.

Calling the day you got an animal the "lucky day" or the "adoption day" isn't some form of denial. When you pick out an animal at the shelter or inherit someone else's pet, there can be a fair amount of baggage—all the stuck thoughts, feelings, and behaviors of the last family. By allowing the animal to stay in that state and coddling it, you aren't really setting the tone you want. You may in fact be denying who it really is.

Memories: Death Makes Angels of All of Us

One woman had me talk to her dog. She was convinced that there was something wrong with her, but she didn't tell me that part. She walked into the session with a cute, bouncy, not-quite-two-year-old Portuguese water dog (a breed that always reminds me of someone whose pajamas are too big).

When I connected with the dog, a few things came up. She told me that she would never be as good as the dog before her, who had died. The husband called her "stupid," and she tried and tried to connect with their kid—and even to take care of him—but for some reason, this was close to impossible. And the dog *knew* that the woman needed her help but felt as if she were failing in that department, so she became a clown.

The woman confirmed that the husband did call the dog stupid and she was clinging to the idea that the old animal was so much easier to deal with. In addition to all that going against the dog, the child was autistic and didn't connect with this loving creature.

Once all of this was revealed, the woman told me that she'd come to me thinking that her pet had attention deficit disorder (ADD), but now she recognized how brilliant and perceptive the dog was. This understanding of old thought patterns that the woman was attaching to the dog changed things instantaneously for the better.

Many people don't even mean to hold on to the memory of the last dog, cat, horse, or bird. And the last thing we want to do is hinder the blooming of this new being in our homes—yet, accidentally, that's often the first thing we do.

Gail and Charlie

Charlie was a small, white, fluffy dog. He was cute but so shy that he'd cower in the corner when people came over to his house, and then he would bark incessantly. This behavior wasn't conducive to a friendly home; he certainly wasn't receptive to humans or other dogs. And if asked to be nice to cats—forget about it. Basically, Charlie was an incorrigible barking machine, especially when it came to the feline species.

This wasn't exactly a harmonious situation, and Gail, Charlie's guardian, was at her wit's end. Who wants to arrive home to that or have people over? While the dog had come into the household with his own issues from his previous home (yes, he was a "rescue"), he told me that he would never measure up to Gail's deceased dog, and that he really did understand the purpose of cats in a household.

Gail and I reframed the whole picture. We talked about not feeling sorry for Charlie because of the emotional damage in his past and instead seeing him as friendly and in harmony with the cats in the house. We talked about what the other dog was like, but emphasized that Charlie now had the opportunity to be something else . . . something just as important, but different. We all should take this to heart: *The new animal will never be that other one, but it may be bringing an element to our lives that we need—something that's just as important as what the previous one did.*

A year or so later, the woman sent me an e-mail saying that Charlie was very happy. He was now friendly with neighbors and even guests, and he tolerated the cats. In short, he had become her best friend.

We can have sympathy for an animal, but there's nothing wrong with setting a time limit. When our pets have been grieving for so long after the loss of another member of the household, a lot of times I'll tell people to put a cap on it. I might say that for the next week and a half we get to go to the depths of grief, but then starting next Thursday at 5 P.M., we'll head in another direction in order to honor the spirit of the lost animal, who would want us to be fully engaged in life.

Deep-Seated Belief Systems

Whether it's a health challenge or an emotional or a behavioral one, a label can dominate the thoughts and feelings around the subject. Staying focused on the outcome we want is an important component. As evident as thoughts and memories are, we don't realize how much we're communicating from our deep-seated belief systems. In fact, we may not be aware of just how deep they go or even *what* they are. Being willing and open can set the tone in the household, thus communicating something entirely different from what animals have been experiencing up to this point.

Some people would rather be right than work out a solution. Sadly, the "rightness" around an event anchors in a result that involves very little change. When we hang on to being correct or defend how we've always done something, the only shift that occurs is in the opposite direction from the one we were intending.

Gabrielle and Me

Chris Bennings is a horse trainer in Fort Lauderdale whom I met through a mutual client. We ended up working together several times. After a few weeks, I noticed a trend: All the horses seemed to *love* him. So I asked him to come up where I ride and give me a dressage lesson on my horse.

"But don't you have two horses?" he inquired.

"Yes, but I'll only be having a lesson on one of them," I replied.

He insisted, "But you have *two* horses. . . ."

"Well, every trainer has given up on the other horse, so I just ride her out on the trails," I said firmly. I was talking about Gabrielle, an Arabian mare and, I might add, an Aries. Between her breeding and her astrological sign, she is "double fire." (Aries is the warrior archetype.) I'm a Leo, and I too am fire. We can get into a battle of wills like no other. She helps me with my basic animal-communication class, we ride on the trails together, and she is gorgeous—until I met Chris, those had been her roles. In the past, she made it abundantly clear that she wasn't interested in dressage by cantering backward in a parking lot with me on her. I now refer to that move as her moonwalk.

Chris came up and somehow talked me into riding Gabrielle during a lesson. I thought, *Well, this will show him—he'll never ask for that again.* She did her usual circus act, cantering sideways, bucking . . . just being hateful about doing anything I'd ask her to do.

When I got off, Chris said gleefully, "She's cool."

"Cool?"

"She's so talented and a great mover." On and on he went. That was certainly one way to look at it. *I actually had to take a step back.* His bottom line about her? She was "athletic." Talk about having to reframe a picture!

When I first got Gabrielle, she would try with all her heart to learn quickly and do the right thing, but then she became chronically lame. No vet could find the cause. Dozens of x-rays with no diagnosis and six horse trainers later . . . forget it. She's "cool"? She's "athletic"? *I* always thought so, but until Chris, nobody shared that belief. This was a first.

She and I shared a deep-seated belief that we would have a fight in the ring, so I enjoyed the trail rides and the long-lining technique (a training method used prior to attaching a cart to the horse for driving). In fact, I almost bought her a cart, thinking, *All right, this would be a fun hobby for us—one without the impact of my weight on her body.* I just didn't want to fight anymore. Additionally, we've been in dressage barns, where Arabs definitely aren't traditionally seen as dressage horses . . . so she's gotten messages from trainers, vets, and the other boarders and horses (the warmbloods) in various facilities.

Whether you want to say that after 12 years we just got it, we had an overnight miracle, or we worked through a lot of karma, now we *do* enjoy the riding discipline of dressage together most days, and she *is* so athletic. When I ask for something, she offers it up—beautifully. We still have our work cut out for us (she'll occasionally do the moonwalk), but there are some days she does certain advanced moves better than my other horse, Rollie, who loves his work and takes it very seriously.

I had helped so many other people with their deep-seated belief systems, but the task between Gabrielle and me had seemed impossible. She has proven to me that *anything* is possible. A relationship can switch seemingly overnight. I call Gabrielle the "12-year overnight sensation"!

Peeling Off the Labels

Chris always asks, "How many people are paying board on horses that everyone else has dismissed as hopeless?" How many dogs are behind fences that are called vicious? How many cats are deemed insufferable? How many birds are referred to as mean? How many kids are labeled troublemakers? (Oh, how the nuns had a field day with *me!*) How many owners are called incompetent? How many times a day do we brand someone with big, bad words?

Trainers will so often tell you, "This is too much horse for you," or "You're never going to get your dog to accomplish that." As long as your safety isn't jeopardized, rather than look for another horse or dog, look for a different trainer. Get a second opinion. Find someone who supports your belief system: You have a right to have those big dreams and the space to set the tone for you and your animal to achieve them.

Cindy called me because her horse just wasn't cutting it. She had a barn full of great barrel racers, and she'd convinced herself that this one horse just didn't want to do it. But he *liked* barrel racing. I got a sense that he was truly a late bloomer. Work was fun, but he wanted to know why he had to do it all the time.

He was naturally talented, so if Cindy could just take her mind out of the equation and make the process more fun, this would be a breeze for him. She had a tough time doing so, as many of the other horses followed her mental track. Because she had a knack for finding competitive animals who loved this sport, she had a lot at stake. This horse was providing her with a sense of failure so strong that she couldn't get past her belief that he couldn't hack it. Then she'd get out there with him and he'd fulfill that negative prophecy.

When we had our session, we talked a lot about her belief system surrounding him and how she had to get her mind out of the way. So the next barrel race, she spent her time in the warm-up ring and even in the starting box, saying out loud: "La, la, la, la, la, la . . ." She was like a little kid, blocking out her own negative mental chatter. It also set such a fun, creative tone that the horse leaped out of the box as the race began, and they had their best time ever!

I met a gorgeous but timid American bulldog. Her owner loved her, but was he very pained by an earlier experience: She'd killed another dog who was trying to get up on his wife's lap. The bulldog now was kept away from the couple's other two little dogs. As the man said, "We're all in prison over this."

He and his wife loved the dog yet couldn't forgive her and were fearful for the safety of the other animals—just an innocent run across the room could potentially trigger another deadly action. The deep-seated belief, the memory all of the painful feelings attached to that incident, and the inability to know what was the right thing to do were indeed imprisoning all of them.

I can only hope that they found a loving way to be free from that prison and have set a different tone for themselves and their animal companions. They needed to accept the situation as a one-in-a-million fluke and forgive the dog on a deep level. Also, they might have benefited from gaining more understanding about breed-specific behaviors and working with a professional trainer. But most important, they needed to understand that somehow they all were part of a bigger contract, so to speak, one that created the situation: Somehow the little dog had completed its process here on planet Earth, and the bulldog was simply facilitating that.

Circus Cats

Another deep-seated belief was uprooted for all the Americans on that trip I made to central Europe with my mother. The first night, the tour director, Richard, who was Polish, asked what I did for a living. When I told him, he was very quiet for a moment. Then he asked, "Have you ever seen trained cats?"

"You mean like trained big cats in the circus?" I responded.

"No, trained house cats in the circus." When I smiled but shook my head no, he informed us that we were in for a treat. He added an extra activity for the tour group that night—we would be going to the circus in Budapest, where we would see trained house cats.

Now I personally know that my cat and I have trained each other, and after working with thousands of clients and their animals, I'm aware that cats *can* be trained, but this was a sight to see.

Watching these cats as they danced, jumped, and performed their routines to perfection was just fantastic and indescribable. For the other Americans sitting in the audience, the performance removed the perception that cats do only what they want. After each cat executed its piece, it would sit there in full glory, absorbing the amusement and enjoyment of hundreds of people as they clapped. Some of the cats were so mesmerized by the delight of the audience that the trainer had to repeatedly call their names to get them off the stage!

Even though the cat trainer spoke in Hungarian and I didn't know the actual words she was saying, she had so much expectancy, authority, and respect all at the same time. Clearly she had a strong vision as well. She set the tone, and those cats just carried it out with delight.

If you have trouble wrapping your brain around the idea that you can train a cat, it's worth a trip to Budapest just to see that it *can* be done!

Through these stories, you can see the wonderful lessons everyone gets to learn, myself included, from communicating with animals. Some weeks my sessions share a theme: aggression, liver disease, release to the next life, feeling unloved, coming to terms with respecting oneself, and so forth. Occasionally, emotions, words, and pictures come into my awareness, and I have to research or learn their symbolic meaning. The animals I work with are obviously blessed because someone took the time to go and seek out an answer.

Many of you are fortunate enough to have that perfect animal companion, but others may be seeing a component in these stories that sounds familiar in your own home. Part I of the book explained why and how these dynamics might arise in your relationships. Part II will give you the tools to help you become adept at communicating with your animals in order to make life better for *all* of you.

❖ ❖ ❖ ❖

PART II

You as the Animal Communicator

❖ Chapter Seven ❖

CREATIVE TOOLS

*If there are no dogs in heaven, then
when I die I want to go where they went.*
— Will Rogers

I can talk to animals until I'm blue in the face, but the most important component of communication is what humans then *do* with the information. Certainly there can be an enormous shift when an animal in a chaotic scenario has gotten a story off its chest. Sometimes the shift in the household or barn occurs because the people have downloaded all of *their* locked emotions around a challenge and are able to reframe the picture. There's nothing like dumping old files from the memory bank in order to move on.

After years of this work and having been exposed to a variety of cases, I've created several tools to enhance that process. I've also used well-known techniques and tailored them to the specific situation at hand. Ultimately, though, the continuation of old behavior versus arriving at a harmonious place comes down to awareness on the guardian's part.

As I've already discussed, it's very difficult to get some pictures, memories, and experiences out of our own cellular memory or our subconscious. When we're so locked into these memories or beliefs, it becomes even more difficult to translate what we want for and from our beloved animals. These tools are designed to help all of the players in this game win.

Job Descriptions and Titles

A job title or description that embodies an animal's essence can bring about stability—or bring out nobility—faster than anything else. It aids in giving your pets a sense of purpose. It's like recognizing their souls' intention, or else co-creating a new one with them. We all do better when we sit down and create a mission statement or have a goal for achieving something. Job descriptions or titles are flexible: This week a grieving dog may need to go back to being the Jokester again, or the Wild One in the household may need to manage the living room while you're gone, instead of destroying furniture.

Inventing job descriptions can be a creative endeavor. Archetypes—such as Clown, Entertainer, Sentry, Overseer of All, Queen, King, Hero, Takeover Artist, and the like—are a powerful tool to give animals a title that's contrary to the negative behavior they're exhibiting. Even the shyest creature has a hero somewhere inside, and even the most aggressive animal has a softy lying dormant within. Job descriptions can be used to develop the hidden part of your pets that you know is in there. For example, help a timid cat come out from under the bed by saying, "I need a Hero [or Sentry or Mascot] here."

I know many a client who has coaxed a shy cat out of its shell with that simple technique. Others have quelled the fear in their timid dog. On the opposite end of that spectrum, I have a horse, Rollie, who was a tough guy when I first got him. Deep down, though, he was really a mama's boy. That title worked for a while in order to get him out of his bad-boy routine. For the first year, it was great to have him depend on me, but when a horse 17 hands high tries to get in your right-hand pocket because he's afraid of the wind, you have a problem. It's even worse when your right-hand pocket is in your pants . . . which you're wearing while on his back. He got a more appropriate title: I began calling him my Knight in Shining Amour. It worked like a charm. When we're riding, we're Fred and Ginger—a dance team—but on the ground, he's the valiant Knight.

Top-Ten List

The top-ten list, which details the ten things we love most about our pets, can move animals' energy faster than anything else, reminding us of who they were to us at one time, and reminding *them* of who they could be. If the list is hung on a stall gate, a refrigerator door, or next to the computer at work, it can act like a subliminal-messaging service for your mind.

Laurel and Grey Man

Grey Man was an Arabian in a dressage barn in Wood-inville, Washington. He was gorgeous but not known for his work ethic. I'd talked to about ten horses at his barn, and Grey Man was the last one. It was already nightfall, and it was cold and wet. His owner, Laurel, didn't really seem interested in what her horse was saying and was agitated about their whole relationship. I could see that they were clearly locked into a pattern. She finally asked me why he got spooked so much. I got quiet, and he really poured his heart out, first betraying a feeling of sadness and then one of failure.

I told her, "Deep down, he really meant to be your hero, and he has completely failed you. He helped you through a lot in your life, yet you're always frustrated with him." Enough said.

Normally, with something as potentially dangerous as spooking, there are a number of specific measures to take. Instead, however, I told Laurel, "I want you to e-mail me a list of the top ten reasons why Grey Man is a hero."

She looked at me like I was cuckoo. "Grey Man a hero? *Ha!* He's anything but a hero—I can't even walk outside without him being spooked by his own shadow."

"Here's my e-mail address. I look forward to hearing how Grey Man is a hero."

Six months later I finally got the e-mail from her. She'd completed the task. The first few items were rather pedestrian and verged on making fun of me for even coming up with this kooky idea, but from about number six on, we were cooking with gas. One of the last four items on the list was along the lines of: "He was my best friend during my divorce." The list was fantastic!

Grey Man also had a lameness that was limiting his dressage work, and he needed a time-out. Laurel also informed me in the e-mail that she realized how much she loved him and that she'd be putting him out to pasture temporarily until the lameness healed. She'd be seeing him less, but she thought that he would be happier.

Then about six months after that, I got another e-mail: Laurel couldn't resist hanging out with Grey Man once she had a clearer view of their relationship. She started trail-riding him, which is something she never would have had the courage to do before because of his spooking. Not only was he excellent out on the trails, but if people approached, he'd sidestep toward the bushes and wait until they passed. She said that she'd overhear passersby say things such as, "What a perfect gentleman!" For a few years after this, I continued to hear nothing but heroic tales of Grey Man.

On the next page is an example of a top-ten list from a client in Kansas.

TOP 10 REASONS WHY ZANZIBAR IS THE GREATEST DOG IN THE WHOLE WIDE WORLD

1. Zan is a lover. He's a sweet guy who gives me kisses and cuddles with me on the floor.

2. Zan is so handsome. He "dresses sharp," keeping himself clean and always looking great. His eyes are bright and beautiful.

3. Zan is smart. He excelled in obedience and agility classes. At home he's observant and pays attention to what's going on. Nothing gets past him!

4. Zan is protective. He's big and strong. I feel safer having him around the house, knowing people can be intimidated by the way he looks.

5. Zan loves getting exercise and being social with other dogs. He also enjoys being "out on the town" with his little sister Vanna and me.

6. Zan adapts to change. Our lives are always going to be shifting, and although sometimes it's hard, Zan takes it in stride. We recently moved, and he has settled in so well at our new home.

7. Zan is fun. He loves to "hide" under towels and play with toys. He really enjoys life!

8. Zan knows how to relax. He strikes a good balance of activity and rest, which makes him easy to live with. He loves curling up by my feet when I'm reading a book or watching TV.

9. Zan is forgiving. I didn't know anything about dogs when I got him, and I learned many things the hard way. Taking care of him has taught me so much. He has never held a grudge about the things I've done wrong. He gives me unconditional love.

10. Zan is reliable. He's there every day to greet me at the door when I get home from work. He lends me a strong shoulder to cry on when things don't go my way. He accepts me for who I am and gives me unconditional support.

Zan, thanks for being such a wonderful dog and adding so much to my life. I love you so much.
— Claire

The top-ten list is great for any circumstance. One woman had given up the horse of her dreams because it was time for him to retire. She got another, which should have been great, but it wasn't the same connection. So we did the top-ten list of how this new horse had gotten into her heart. This sealed their fate of being a loving team.

Another great use for the top-ten list, which I've recommended time and time again with much success, is when a new animal comes into a household and tries to take the number one position from an existing animal. It's common for the newbie to come in and say, "Move over. I'm so cute. I'm the new one everybody is paying attention to. *I'm* the star now."

The existing number one animal can have any of a number of reactions, but if it doesn't fight to retain its position, this is a great reminder to everyone why that animal is number one. Perhaps the word *pacifist* should appear somewhere on the top-ten list as a reminder to all concerned that going about things peacefully is a noble way to approach every situation.

Hierarchy List

Always list yourself highest in the hierarchy—you, your spouse, and other adults go on top equally, followed by kids, then animals. The list of animals' positions should be in order of appearance, as in who came into the home first. Again, when new pets enter the household and have a "Takeover Artist" archetype coursing through their veins, this is a great way to show them where they truly fall in the family.

Just as a side note, kids *always* have to go above the animals. This is particularly true if children come along in a household where a dominant animal has lived for years. As babies become toddlers, they frequently chase or poke animals (as youngsters do). The hierarchy list helps pets remember to be tolerant . . . or to be young again and jump out of the way!

Schedules and Calendars

A schedule is also a great thing for a young animal in training, especially for the supersmart, super-scattered types. For dogs and cats, this schedule can go by the food bowl or even on the refrigerator. For horses, it can go on the stall door (or in the tack room if they're out to pasture). And if you're like me and your car is your part-time office, put the schedule on the passenger seat so that you're constantly reminded of it.

You automatically send animals the picture—it's etched in stone, and you can stop doubting whether you have a plan.

Karen and Kellogg

Kellogg was a type A personality, a thoroughbred who was at the track for eight years. (Most horses don't stay there that long unless they were fantastic and/or they enjoy the sport.) Karen was a type A personality in marketing and sales. She traveled around the world teaching courses to large corporations. Together, Karen and Kellogg were doing hunter-jumpers (a division of English riding that judges the movement of the horse and the coordination of the horse and rider). He carried an air about him that seemed to say, *Why bother going in the show ring unless you're going to win?*

At some point Kellogg started bucking. The first thing I do with bucking is scan the body to see if there's pain. Horses—just like people—can benefit from a chiropractic adjustment when they work at this competitive level. But nothing stood out that would warrant this sudden behavior. Being the winner type meant he was also a perfectionist in every way, so needless to say, he was a *good* bucker. It wasn't safe for Karen or the trainer to ride him. On my visit, I asked Kellogg why he was doing this.

He was so confused about his life and its direction. At the time, he (like Karen) needed goals. Sometimes he would ride with the trainer, and other times he would ride with Karen. To make matters worse, people would come by and say, "Poor Kellogg—Karen must be out of town." Yet then that very day she might show up. There were mixed messages coming from every direction. He doubted whether Karen really ever left town, and he wondered what was wrong with him that everyone was saying "Poor Kellogg."

So I suggested that Karen post two months of her schedule on the stall wall so that it was clear to anyone peering in whether she was in town and coming to ride or was out of the state or the country teaching and Kellogg would be ridden by the trainer. Every business trip had to be recorded. That way people wouldn't wonder anymore whether Karen would be around: It was there in black and white. During the session, we got clarity on how many shows were coming up—Kellogg had something to look forward to, and his own life was no longer a mystery.

Special Acknowledgments

Merlin was a superstar in his day, and in the plan to phase him out of competition and into retirement, he was being used as a school horse. The problem was that he was bucking and scaring the young students. I went straight to his body first and found nothing out of the ordinary. (His person is a gifted healer, so I didn't think that was the problem—but I always check.) I asked if he liked teaching. He said that he really did but that nobody knew who he was. He didn't feel special and wasn't acknowledged for the superstar he had been.

I suggested putting a star on his stall so that everyone who was new would have to ask about it and thus would hear his story . . . or they would just get the subliminal message that they were fortunate enough to be learning from this master. Merlin stopped terrifying new students!

Merlin the Star.

Another story that demonstrates the importance of acknowledgment is that of a woman who called me because her superstar agility dog had just blown a big contest. We discovered that he was competing for her sake, which was fine, but he knew that deep down she wasn't doing it for the fun of it. The dog was aware that she had way too much invested in gaining approval from her father. Winning for her had nothing to do with what she and the dog were doing together and everything to do with proving herself. I suggested that she make him a certificate of appreciation, because this lesson was more valuable than any trophies or ribbons could have been. Now they go to agility trials for fun (and they just so happen to win!).

By way of acknowledgment, sometimes it's fun to dress up your animals, put a dot on their head, or do things to signal their changed state to you and your household.

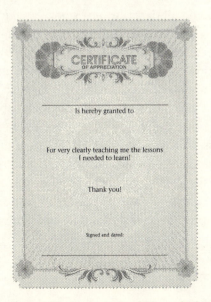

A Certificate of Appreciation is a fun and useful form of acknowledgment.

Parties and Celebrations

I've had many clients throw retirement parties for their performance animals. It's great to really go all out for them. Pull out the awards and the pictures, review the memories, make a speech, put on leis . . . just go crazy! Have your friends over—human friends, cat friends, horse friends—and just brag. Be sure to include any new members of the household, particularly up-and-coming show animals. Make sure they know exactly who the celebrated animals are and how gracefully they will retire into the home.

A retirement party doesn't work just for performance animals. I've had many people host one when an animal has always been "on duty"—perhaps around a farm—and won't relax. Sometimes, on-duty animals are also the ones who take on everything emotional that's going on in *your* life. An easy remedy for this is to have a party, acknowledging all that they've done as ascended beings, but showing that now they get to enjoy the life in the particular species' body in which they've been incarnated.

I boarded horses at a barn in Los Angeles for ten years. It didn't take much for us to find an excuse to have a party, but the best one of all was the "baby shower" before my horse Pony Boy was born. I opened the presents for his mother, Pet One! We all ate a mean carrot cake I make that's good for both people and horses.

Personally, I don't think that you need to have an excuse for a party—how about just throwing one because you want to enjoy your animal companions with your friends and theirs?

I got great gifts at Pony Boy's baby shower.

Joan's Carrot Cake for People and Horses

1½ cups sugar
1¼ cups coconut oil or organic unsalted butter, melted
2 teaspoons vanilla extract
4 eggs, lightly beaten
2 cups all-purpose flour, sifted
2 teaspoons baking soda
1 teaspoon sea salt
3 teaspoons cinnamon
½ teaspoon nutmeg
3 cups shredded carrots

Preheat oven to 375°F. Combine the sugar, oil or melted butter, and vanilla extract. Beat in the eggs. Combine the baking soda, salt, cinnamon, and nutmeg; and stir gradually into the oil mixture. Add the carrots, pour batter into a greased cake pan, and bake for 45 minutes.

Sometimes it's fun to make cupcakes instead: Frost some for the people, and leave those for the animals plain.

Visualization

Visualization is a key to harmony in a household, as well as to enhancing performance in the show ring. It's even wonderful for healing illnesses or lameness. If you're at work thinking that your cat will pee on the carpet or that your dog will dig up the begonias, it's like hitting the e-mail "Send" button on your computer. Actively visualizing the opposite scenario will create the picture you *want:* that of the cat using the litter box, the dog running in the backyard to burn off excess energy, and so on.

My brother for many years enjoyed the life of a world-class "extreme snowboarder," a title that he earned after being one of the first people to snowboard down the peaks of Valdez in Alaska. Since then he has jumped out of many helicopters for commercials and movies. If you were to ask him how he did what he did, he'd be quick to say that on the ride up, he had to "see" what line he'd take through the untouched snow to get down safely—with minimal avalanches.

Once he was on top of the mountain, the vantage point was very different from what it had been looking down from the helicopter, but the line he had already created in his head led him down each time. He rarely veered from the already-seen path, even though things looked totally different going down.

Likewise, many sports figures or athletic teams have gathered to play the game in their minds together before they get to the field or stadium. Part of the magic is the individual or group setting the intention. Why wouldn't this be the same for us with our animals?

If you have a long drive after work from your job to the barn where you ride, why not prepare yourself during this car trip? Or perhaps as you're grooming your horse, you can see in your mind what it is you hope to accomplish on your ride: Maybe it's a safe journey down a thickly wooded trail or the execution of a triple combination jump. Perhaps it's getting around the barrel fast enough to increase your time. Maybe it's imagining yourself sitting more correctly so that your horse glides sideways across the arena in a dressage test, or saying out loud to your jockey (with the horse within hearing range) how you see him blowing the socks off of the other horses in the race.

If you're a dog person, your visualizations could involve seeing the dog carry out each of the activities in the obedience ring easily and effortlessly. In an agility or tracking trial, perhaps you imagine the whole test before it happens, focusing on your connection as the dog continues through the course of events with speed and precision.

If you're someone who's showing your dog or your horse, speaking the vision out loud can be very effective. This is especially important if you don't trust your visualization to transfer or you don't feel as if you're a very visual person. Rather than socializing with other people at the event, take the time with your partner to discuss what you will do in the class or trial. Again and again I tell people that speaking out loud only reinforces the pictures. Send them the double image from your mind and your words. Perhaps you can still the nerves you both may have through speaking this in a calm tone.

This is also something to really concentrate on if you're sitting at work worrying about the family dynamics at home. If your pets aren't getting along, imagine all your dogs lying on the rug next to you on the couch or your cats curled up on the bed together. Visualize the dogs and cats touching nose to nose. *Seeing is believing.* If the behavior at home isn't what you want it to be, every time that you think of how it is, reframe the picture to create what you want. This is a very powerful tool—animals *do* see your pictures. If you've established how things *should* unfold, go back to the image that you created.

It's not cheating to pull out photos of your pets in a more harmonious time and allow them to be visible while you're reprogramming your own brain. Wallpaper your office with images displaying how cute they were together at one time! Again, this serves as a reminder for you to hold that vision for them.

Affirmations

Pictures click off in your head as you speak. Affirmations are really for *you,* and creating them in a singsong or an upbeat tone can get you out of your own head, away from that place of doubt.

An important component of making up a strong affirmation is assuring that it's in the positive. Your subconscious mind—and the animals who are receptive to what's in it—can't break down grammatical constructions such as *don't* or *can't.* If you say, "Don't dig in the yard," both your subconscious mind and the animal are only going to see the picture of the dog digging in the yard.

Back in the '80s, a guy friend of mine had a brutal breakup with his girlfriend of seven years. He told me then that he didn't want another heartbreak and that mentally he was putting a red circle with a slash through the word *relationship* so that he didn't attract one. Of course, girls looking for a romantic connection were drawn to him. Finally, a rather hip therapist told him that his subconscious mind couldn't comprehend the red circle with a slash through it, and he was attracting more of the subject dominating his thought: that is, a relationship.

It's the same with animals. Rather than saying "Don't dig in the yard," make up an affirmation about how "Buddy loves to sit peacefully in the garden." The phrase must reflect the *positive* behavior.

I had a client who lived on a greenbelt in Denver. Coyotes and other creatures were known to roam through this suburban neighborhood. Her cat was very savvy. However, her husband feared for this little creature's life, and his anxiety was making the cat resistant to coming home. I suggested giving the cat boundaries, whereby he had to be in at 6 every night and then he could have dinner. I had my client take up all the food bowls during the day (it's better for animals' digestion not to free-feed anyway). We worked on a singsong-type affirmation, using positive words only—not "You had better come inside or dinner is denied," but rather, "The cat obeys the rules and is in by 6 P.M." Again, it wasn't a phrase about no dinner because that would have played out as "You had better come in (and even if you don't, you still get to have your dinner)."

For timid animals, people have used the affirmation "You are always safe with me, and there is a whole world to see."

By making the affirmation whimsical and fun, it also takes the negative emotion—which has previously fueled the communication between you and the animal—out of the equation, meaning that if you're frustrated because your cat has peed on the couch, the affirmation can't be grumbling about your companion using the litter box. If, on the other hand, you invented a song about how much "We love the litter box" and made it more fun for the cat to *want* to please you, suddenly there's a whole different energy around the housebreaking process.

A lot of people are timid about riding their horse after an accident even though they know their animal is sorry. Perhaps on the day when you're going to just get back on for the first time, you could make up a little song about walking safely around the arena.

Remember the story in the last chapter about my dog-agility teacher telling the class members to always have a smile on their faces while doing training? When the frustration goes up, the intelligence goes down—and the intention goes right out the window. Maybe you feel dumb taking a singsong approach to affirmations, but who's listening anyway? Besides, think of how powerful it was when Mary Poppins got Jane and Michael Banks to clean their room by singing a song and making it fun!

Holly and Pippi

Pippi is probably the best illustration I've encountered of the power of affirmations at work. Holly called from Wisconsin for a phone session. Pippi, a border collie, lived with her, her husband, a shepherd mix who was about ten, and a five-year-old golden retriever. Pippi herself was about two and a half at the time and hadn't been with the family for very long.

I tuned in to Pippi, and many revelations later, it became obvious that the dog had had a rough beginning.

In her present situation, the older German shepherd seemed to be the Goddess/Matriarch of the farm who took care of everything. The five-year-old Lab was akin to a tub overflowing with love for humans and dogs alike. Pippi acted like a scaredy-cat and barked incessantly at people—and probably frightened off more than a few folks! (I find that most people don't stop to determine which type of bark they're hearing by considering, *Gee, is this a fear bark or a sign of aggression?*) So this was truly unwanted behavior.

When I got on the phone with Holly, I explained that Pippi didn't want to be a scaredy-cat, but that there were several things going on that fueled her behavior:

1. She didn't have a real job because they were all taken.

2. She was very unsure of herself due to her turbulent beginnings.

3. She knew that Holly and her husband weren't certain whether or not to keep her because she didn't really fit in.

Holly told me that Pippi was afraid of, and barked at, the farm help (especially men), the UPS man . . . anyone and everyone—so we acknowledged how she behaved and that it was the opposite of the confident, at-home dog she wanted to be. Then we reframed the picture based on the desired outcome. I suggested that Pippi be given the job of Apprentice to the Goddess/Matriarch of the farm. Since that dog was ten, Pippi would be needed to run the farm eventually because the Lab was about love and fun and wouldn't be able to handle things as the shepherd had.

A border collie not having an occupation is close to being one of the worst offenses on planet Earth: And here Pippi was third in the pack, with both the good jobs (running the joint and providing love) already taken. That's a very difficult position for any dog to be in, but it's especially so for a border collie.

So I asked Holly if she and her husband could see Pippi as the Apprentice rather than a scaredy-cat. She said that they probably could. I explained that sometimes maintaining the new vision can be challenging for people because the past behavior will frequently be juxtaposed with the picture they're trying to hold in their heads.

I told Holly, "I'm going to give you some affirmations for you *and* Pippi. But first I need to hear your 'Good dog, Pippi' voice."

So Holly spoke in a higher tone, saying, "Good dog, Pippi."

I said, "Okay, keep the Pippi voice and repeat after me: 'Pippi loves the UPS man.'" She repeated the new phrase. We went through all the people who came to work at the farm and created a whole script about how much Pippi loved them.

Then (Divinely timed, of course) Holly excaimed, "Oh my God, you're never going to believe this, but the UPS man is coming down the walkway toward the house!"

I said, "Don't panic—put the phone down and do the affirmations."

Holly set down the receiver, and in her silly "Good dog, Pippi" voice stood there greeting the UPS man and speaking to Pippi about how much she loved him, how fun it is that he comes to visit, blah, blah, blah—a stream of consciousness all about Pippi, love, and the UPS man.

Pippi didn't bark . . . apparently she even got a little smell of the guy and backed away. Off the UPS man went, happy that he wasn't threatened by Pippi's fearful barking. Holly came back on the line: She couldn't believe it.

Since then, the combination of Pippi being able to tell her story, acknowledging that she was heartbroken from the past and lacked a current job; reframing the picture of her as the Apprentice to the Goddess/Matriarch of the farm; and creating some affirmations for the specific places where there was complete breakdown in communication prior to the consultation has created a really welcome home and a fulfilling place for Pippi to be. She also fulfills her breed-specific need of being a full-time working dog!

Within an hour, Pippi's circumstances had been changed forever. She continues to thrive and has even gotten to know the farm helpers. Holly and her husband's commitment to helping Pippi succeed should also be commended. It seemed kind of wacky to say "We love the UPS man," but in truth, what's wackier: letting a dog remain out of sorts in life, or saying silly phrases that can be life altering?

Pippi (left) missed out on all the taken jobs.

Prayer

Praying is one of the most important things you can do. I know that when I'm in trouble, scared, or out of balance, that's the first thing I turn to. But there were times in the past when my habit was to freak out about a situation or try to control it. After enough pretty rough experiences, I now know that I'm Divinely taken care of.

Sometimes things happen so that we can learn to put our attention on God and away from ourselves—or in order to remind us to get back in that state of One Mind. If you have an aging or ill animal companion, don't forget the prayer along with glucosamine or the power meds.

A lot of us have mental blocks or feel awkward about the religion we were raised with and attach that feeling to prayer, but this needn't be. Sometimes simple mantras are appropriate—I have a lot of them! If you do have a particular prayer from your childhood that resonates with you, shout it out. Don't be shy!

MANTRAS

- *Om.* A sacred Hindu syllable, om has a long *o* sound: Enjoy it as much as the extended *Mmm . . .*

- *Om Shanti, Shanti, Shanti.* This translates to "Om, peace, peace, peace."

- *Lord Jesus Christ, have mercy on me.* This is known to Christians as the Jesus Prayer. Inhale on the first phrase; exhale on the second.

- *Be still, and know that I am God.* This is a verse from the Psalms of the Old Testament.

- *Shalom.* This is the Hebrew word for "peace."

- *Bismillah al-Rahman al-Rahim.* An Islamic prayer from the Koran, this translates to "In the name of Allah, the Compassionate, the Merciful."

There's a book called *The Way of the Pilgrim* that tells of a man in Russia who walks all around the country and teaches that repeating the Jesus Prayer over and over brings you to a euphoric state daily. The idea behind repetitive prayers or mantras is that you make them part of your subconscious. Furthermore, they work automatically to raise your frequency. When your frequency is elevated, you're much more available to be of service to someone who's sick or dying without taking everything on yourself.

Sometimes it seems that there are just too many prayers to be answered. In my office, I have two boxes:

(1) immediate prayers and (2) answered prayers. When I hang up from a phone session, or after I've been to a home with a challenging situation, I write down the problem on a Post-it note, date it, and place it in the first prayer box, which is filled with lost animals and seemingly unsolvable illnesses and behaviors.

Every so often I go through the box and notice that some of the prayers have been answered. Immediately those Post-it notes go into the answered-prayers box. I keep the immediate-prayers box next to my desk so that I have easy access to it between phone sessions. The answered-prayers box stays on my bookshelf in front of my desk so that my eyes fall on it regularly throughout a session, reminding me that in any situation—even a seemingly hopeless one—prayers *are* answered.

❖ *Chapter Eight* ❖

TAPPING INTO ONE MIND

The youth walks up to the white horse, to put its halter on
and the horse looks at him in silence.
They are so silent, they are in another world.
— D. H. Lawrence

In my travels I met Eddie Maple, who rode Secretariat and won the horse's final race, which took place at the Canadian International at Woodbine Racetrack in Toronto. (Secretariat had already won the Triple Crown—the Kentucky Derby, the Preakness Stakes, and the Belmont Stakes.) Meeting Eddie stirred a thousand questions in me, and I had to have them answered at once. Eddie obliged.

Eddie told me about the magical day of the race. This was 1973; Watergate was going on, as well as the Vietnam War. Because Secretariat had such a winning spirit, he—like those greats before him, Seabiscuit and Man o' War—mesmerized fans. On that particular rainy, cold day in Ontario, however, Secretariat had much going against him. The fog was so thick that it delayed his last workout before the race. The weather, while daunting, didn't stop more than 30,000 fans from showing up to watch him.

Secretariat's regular jockey, Ron Turcotte, who had triumphed with him in the Triple Crown, was disqualified, so Eddie was picked to ride. This was like a dream come true for him, but needless to say, a lot was at stake in riding the greatest horse in his last race. Also, they would be up against another great horse, the Canadian superstar Kennedy Road.

Eddie knew that Secretariat would either win big or he wouldn't put his heart in it at all. On that day, you could hear a pin drop in the stands. Eddie himself stayed very quiet yet expectant, and that was the demeanor of the whole team as well—the trainer, the owner, *and* Secretariat. . . . And they won the race.

The Power of One Mind

While Eddie and Secretariat's story might seem like an odd way to start out a chapter on One Mind, it isn't at all. To me, this is one of the *best* illustrations of One Mind at work.

Eddie Maple—a young jockey, early in his career, riding a horse with the biggest heart of all for the first time—was linking up with an animal who knew exactly what he was doing. Eddie was working for a trainer and owner who held nothing less than a victorious vision . . . and had the track record to prove it. Secretariat's big heart inspired people to tap into One Mind, his fans and opponents included.

Athletic prowess and good performances are valued in our society. When we see an agility trial and it goes fantastically, our hearts sing. The dog and the human are linked—the animal just flies over the jumps yet mentally checks in with its person, who's staying single-mindedly focused. *They are in One Mind.*

Remember the studies of the mirror neuron that I mentioned in Chapter 2? As spectators, we *all* soar. We *all* experience that triumph. And we all feel for those who gave their all, yet something prevented them from winning. After one of the Triple Crown races, even Secretariat's owner, Penny Tweedy, said that she would have been disappointed if Secretariat hadn't won, but that she would have been happy for a rival horse, Sham, to be the victor because *he* was a great horse. Here she was, the owner of the greatest horse of the last century, yet she said that she always felt bad that the year Sham ran was the same one that Secretariat did.

Secretariat's Triple Crown jockey, Ron Turcotte, has been known to say that he never did anything when he rode him because Secretariat knew what he was doing. At the Belmont Stakes, Secretariat broke from the gates in last place and remained there in the first turn. Still, he won by 31 lengths (approximately 1/16 of a mile) ahead of any of the other horses. After he won what's already a long race and set a new record, the horse continued to run faster down the track for another eighth of a mile to break yet *another* record! He had a stride that was said to be 25 feet long. After the race, Ron Turcotte was quoted as saying, "He was running easy."

This was a horse who led the One Mind movement. His owner had won him in a coin toss, and the trainer wasn't sure in the beginning that there was much to work with. But in no time, Secretariat turned the vision of each and every person who came into his life into victory.

COMMUNICATION WITH ALL LIFE

A victory in our daily lives doesn't always mean the prestige, glory, and cash involved with high-stakes racing. Sometimes it's just getting through the day. Ultimately, connecting to One Mind aids in hearing the responses from our animals—whether we're ready to do so or not! By learning from those who connect in One Mind, we can better understand the power and force behind it.

Gerry, Finnigan, and Star

A trainer named Gerry at the racetrack in Denver wanted me to come down to talk to two horses. He picked an odd time of the day so as not to be seen by any of the other trainers. Some racetrack people are still very superstitious, and Gerry certainly didn't want anyone to know what his new leg up was, so to speak. He pointed out which two horses he needed me to talk to. Clearly this wasn't going to be a warm, fuzzy chat about how much love was shared between them. The trainer had an agenda.

"What is it you want to know?" I asked.

Gerry looked at me incredulously a moment, then blurted out, "Why aren't they winning?" with an attitude of *What else is there to ask?*

The first horse, Finnigan, gave me a sense that he always started out strong and had great speed, but halfway through the race it was as though he lost his power. He would get winded.

"Yeah, that's right . . . but *why?*" the trainer demanded. When I checked in with the horse physically, I had a sense that he couldn't breathe after a while. The problem seemed to be in the throat area. There wasn't enough oxygen—in effect, Finnigan lost the wind in his sails. The first part of the race he could depend on the initial breaths he took, but something was obstructing his breath later on.

"Oh, then that's easy—I have one of those special bits. I'll switch it for him," the trainer said. The equipment that Gerry was using was rather standard. With this new information, he suspected that there was an extra flap down the horse's throat that was creating the impediment. Without the expense of medical tests, Gerry was willing to try the different bit.

The next horse, Star, was very clear: He told me that once the starting gate opened, the jockey tended to put him into the middle of the madness: many horse torsos and hooves and dirt flying. Star had vision and space issues and couldn't stand being in the pileup of other animals. Simply put, he needed to be guided around all the horses to the perimeter when they came out of the gate, even though this could cost him time. If he could be on the outside and see the end of the track, he could get there quickly and pass all of the other horses. Star knew exactly what he needed.

"Okay, I'll tell the jockey" was Gerry's response.

A few months later, the trainer called and told me that not only were both horses winning now, but Finnigan had just won by seven lengths. Months later, Gerry took one of my classes and it turns out he was very talented!

Gerry knew his two horses better than anyone else possibly could. As far as personality traits went, I couldn't have told him anything he didn't know. It was that little extra bit of information that he needed in both cases. The one thing he knew for sure was that these two horses were very competitive and could be considered serious contenders at that track. He could feel it, and in his heart, he knew that something very simple yet significant was creating resistance for each horse.

Once Gerry removed that barrier, then he, the jockeys, and each of the horses had a single-minded goal. They were all hooked into One Mind with that intention, allowing the full force of all their respective talents to be ultimately focused on winning. And from there, winning was easy.

Ruth and Max

Another client of mine, Ruth, had been showing her dog, Max, in obedience trials, trying to get to the next title. They had been so fantastic. All of the elements were there: He loved to perform, he was smart, he was a Zen master, and they were a great team. Yet Ruth said that her dog had just checked out in the middle of the class. Why?

When I asked him, Max told me that Ruth was so nervous that there was a certain point when all he could hear was static, and he didn't know what came next. He wasn't connected to her: Her nervousness made her disengaged.

Ruth was a trial lawyer, so I asked her how she approached a trial if she wasn't entirely prepared or certain of the outcome. She said that she walked in with great confidence and stated her case to the judge.

I told her, "That's what you'll have to do here." We incorporated other techniques later, but once Ruth gave this her all, they won. Max was able to mentally tune in

to her confidence, even if she was simply *gesturing* like a
trial lawyer!

Farmers' Intuition

Once I had to speak at the Greeley Farm Show in Colorado. As I drove up, I thought, *Oh, there probably won't
be any people at my lecture—what interest will these farmers
have in knowing about telepathic communication? This isn't
my normal group* . . . on and on went my thoughts. My
usual audience includes more New Age types as well as
dog or horse groups and rescue organizations. This was a
little different for me, but I got over my reservations and
decided that no matter how many people were there, it
would be fun.

To my surprise, the room was packed: All 100 seats
were full, and it was standing room only. To my even
greater surprise, these farmers *got it.* For more than two
hours, they asked the best questions I'd ever heard from
any audience.

So why did they "get it" better than almost every
other group? Because farmers have a common goal with
their animals, and their livelihood is dependent upon
communication, upon everyone working together to get
the job done, and upon all beings connecting to One
Mind for a single-minded goal. The farmers asked questions about their dogs, their horses, their mules, and
so on to ensure that the work would go efficiently. Did
they bring treats and have cute-colored animal halters?
Probably not. Did they share the power of intention with
these animals? Absolutely!

In a departure from my normal talk, I decided that I

would venture out on a limb a bit and get audience members to *try* telepathic communication. We took a break and met in the round pen outside afterward. I had 65 handouts for this part of the event (I'd thought that was way too many), but to my further surprise, people had to share the handouts in groups of two or three. Everyone had come outside to talk to the horse in the round pen—and they had brought friends. The horse was able to remain calm as the minds of all these farmers reached in to pluck an answer or two from him. The images that they described receiving from the horse were crystal clear. Those farmers taught *me* a lesson that day!

Mindfulness

People frequently ask me, "My animal just stares at me—what is he trying to say?" I usually tell them that there may not be anything that he's trying to say; he could simply be hoping to elicit that vital connection with you so that the two of you ultimately tune in to One Mind together, right then and there. This is the opportunity for a momentary glimpse into the Divine.

Now, in this case, you could get quiet and see if you pick up anything. If nothing seems pressing, what a beautiful opportunity just to experience One Mind! To connect with another on this profound level is to tap into the whole. Ultimately, every religion, every spiritual practice, is about getting a sense of this and carrying it with you throughout the day . . . through this life . . . and on to the afterlife. And here your animal companion is, looking you right in the face, offering this to you. What a blessing!

We often get caught up in the "We have to *do* something" mind-set. We go back to our usual human *do*ings rather than acting like human *be*ings. Perhaps the next time your animal companion—or any animal—just stares at you, be still and see it as an opportunity for that One Mind connection.

One Mind or mindfulness is a state of awareness—that feeling of connectedness—something that with practice, we're to carry out in our everyday life. Secretariat, while special at racing, wasn't unique in this respect—*every* animal is offering to pull you toward that vital connection. He was just fortunate in that everyone around him got it; he was lucky that they all happened to have that same agenda. But it was said that he loved people, and my guess is that he offered One Mind to those who just saw him in his stall or playing in a field. Meanwhile, your own cat may be offering this to you from the top of the fridge . . . your turtle may be doing so from inside his tank.

One of my favorite books ever written is *Living Buddha, Living Christ* by Thich Nhat Hanh, a Vietnamese Buddhist monk. In it, he states:

> To me mindfulness is very much like the Holy Spirit. Both are agents of healing. When you have mindfulness, you have love and understanding, you see more deeply, and you can heal the wounds in your own mind. The Buddha was called the King of Healers. In the Bible, when someone touches Christ, he or she is healed. It is not just touching a cloth that brings about a miracle. When you touch deep understanding and love, you are healed.

Separation Anxiety

People often think that because we're pulling out the suitcases, our animal companions know that we're going on a trip and are therefore inclined to act out or are susceptible to depression. Actually, the separation from your animal starts long before the suitcase gets packed and you're out the door. When you're planning something big, frequently you're busy with the details, such as thinking about what time your flight is, arranging for the rental car, and so on. And then suddenly the thought *Oh, and what will the poor dog do while I'm gone?* floats through your mind. The dog picks up on the idea that there might be something wrong with this whole picture, and with your attention geared toward the fine points of what comes next on your trip planning, your animal can't penetrate the minutiae. The luggage is simply confirmation!

This is such a great metaphor for separation from One Mind. We get caught up in the details of life and in the raw emotions that our animals display, so we cater to their immediate needs rather than simply saying, "I'll be back in ten days."

Each day you're away—whether it involves long hours of working or idle exploring—in the quiet of the night, settle into yourself and send a message to your animal. It can be something simple such as, *Just think—in eight more days, I'll be home.* It's important to send a positive image, giving animals something to look forward to.

Moving is the same thing. Animals seem to panic when the boxes come out. Your attention goes to a thousand particulars, between financial details and logistics. But if you continually include your animal friends in the process, taking a moment to verbally walk them through the steps and stages and describing what the new house will be like for them, there's usually a much better transition.

Separation anxiety has a hold on both you and the animal hours before your physical body actually leaves the home. This builds up as you get ready, egging on the unwanted response of anxiety. Stay connected with the animal in One Mind while you're putting on mascara, grabbing your shoes, and guzzling your coffee. Stay tuned to it throughout the day. Allow the mental connection to be part of the link, the safety net, the place the animal connects with if it starts to panic.

This even works for herd-bound horses. Stay single-mindedly focused on the concept that as a leader, you're their connection to One Mind, and allow the security in that fact to help them forget that they left their little buddy in the stall. This will enable them to connect with the activity *you* want.

The Little Ego Voice

One of the main opponents to this connection is the little "ego voice," which can come off in your mind like a big, bad, bratty nuisance. I'm not talking about the wounded-pride ego that's beaten up when you didn't make it through the entire jumping course or your dog was naughty in the show ring. I'm talking about the little voice in your head that *appears* to be helping you out—the one that rips through your mind while you're trying to feed your bird in a hurry before work to warn you of the coming bite that will take flesh off your hand.

It's the voice that invades your mind when you're not paying attention, and suddenly it's the predominant thought. This voice ultimately *prevents* you from getting through the entire jumping course or successfully coaxing your dog to sit on command in front of the judge.

Sometimes this is the voice that appears to be connected to gut instinct. It's a slippery little thing that for some people escalates into a big screaming match with your better instincts, masquerading as something that's trying to act in your best interests. This same little voice can sabotage you, keep you in a safe place in life, and add to any resistance you're harboring. It's the voice that tells you you're having a bad hair day and shouldn't go outside anyway because of the dog's separation anxiety.

The little ego voice is also what prevents One Mind. If you've had an accident on the trail with your horse and you're going to go past the place where the unfortunate event took place, it's the voice that says, "Oh, we can't do that." Then the body responds, the picture appears, and suddenly the horse is picking up on the frenzy.

As I mentioned in Chapter 6, a study at Washington University in St. Louis showed that projecting into the future means borrowing from the mind's memory bank. If we're not aware or are rushing through things, the little ego voice can be what's driving us to the next moment or sequence of events. It's the voice that pipes in and says, "My dog is going to dig in the yard—*again.*"

We're all empathic and are able to pick up on things from others. We can be projecting our ego voice onto others all the time and not even be aware of it. Finding where our inner mute button is can really shift our relationships with our animals (and everyone else)!

The best thing to do with this little voice is to center yourself and say, "Thank you for sharing" and then hold the picture of the behavior that you want. Or state, "I'm deleting that thought—this time my cat will use the litter box." And if that doesn't work, speak compassionately to your little voice, saying, "I know that in the past the cat has done this, but now I'm dumping that file—we have a new way of thinking." Enroll your little ego voice to participate with you in creating the vision of the litter box.

Valerie and Coby

A woman named Valerie called me because at least one of her six cats was peeing around the house. It was making her insane. She and her husband ran a private-investigator firm and had surveillance cameras. She told me she was hooking them up around the house to make sure they could nail down which of her cats was responsible; that way, we could get right to the heart of the matter during our session.

When the appointment time came, Valerie was very distressed that the video footage had revealed that the culprit was her favorite cat ever, her darling Coby. We talked at length with Coby and all of the other animals. Coby's situation was pretty straightforward: He wasn't recognized as the top cat by the others, and when the latest kitten came in a year before, all of the household order went out the window.

I talked to Valerie about how to make Coby feel like things were more organized around the house and what he could be in charge of. Most important, we discussed how she had to stop obsessing about the peeing (which she admitted that she and her husband had been doing) and truly focus on the litter box. I said, "If you're going to obsess about something, focus on all of them—but particularly Coby—easily and effortlessly using the litter box."

A couple of months later, Valerie e-mailed me and the subject line read: "Did you tell Coby to use the toilet?" I picked up the phone immediately to call her and hear *this* story. Apparently things had calmed down, yet one morning she smelled cat pee in one of the bathrooms, so she and her husband set up surveillance cameras there. Sure enough, Coby was using the toilet. They filmed it for many days, and apparently at one point the newest kitten even came in to watch what Coby was doing!

Purity of Spirit

As I mentioned in Chapter 1, animals are definitely clued in to One Mind in a way that we are not. They see us as *part* of the Divine—we aren't separate in their world. Their awareness of One Mind just *is*. It isn't questioned. They don't feel a need to go to confession. They don't engage in wars over their perception of God. It's just accepted and is all-encompassing. In domesticated life, *we* are of One Mind for them, as they are for us. In that respect, we have a lot to learn from them.

Sometimes people grieve so much more over an animal's death than they do over their own family member's. I believe that there are two reasons for this:

1. Animals are living in that One Mind space, and they offer us a purity of spirit in the form of unconditional love. The opportunity to experience it is always available.

With humans, there may have been different aspects to the relationship that weren't all affectionate. With animals, even if there was a behavioral challenge, we could still experience that love.

2. Because the relationship is less contaminated with "stuff," it creates a channel to release the other grief that has lain dormant in our systems, which we didn't have time, or allow ourselves the space, to release.

Animals are more available to just being. Because of that, they sense something without knowing it, just operating from the "fight or flight" principle. They can perceive danger from One Mind. That's the instinct we've shut out, which is the price we pay for the overload of cushy surroundings. The flip side is that we have reason, and that's what we have to offer them. There's a time and a place for instinct *and* reason.

Recently, a film called *The Secret* has taken the world by storm. *The Secret* is based on the Law of Attraction, which says that "like attracts like." It's about not blaming yourself for anything that you previously experienced, because you were unaware of your participation in attracting it. It shows how much better your life can be if you set up it up for positive results . . . in other words, by being in One Mind. Don't forget about the cat trainer at the circus in Budapest, who had an expectation of—and authority over—the outcome, and the cats were able to perform in just that way. Not only can you apply this same principle to your pets, but you can actually watch how *they* apply it themselves.

Our animals expect certain things from us. My dog expects that our walks will be adventures—they always are. My cat expects to have dinner prepared—I always prepare it. My horses expect certain care, and if they don't get it, they demand it in not-so-subtle ways. Some dogs expect to be in trouble. Some expect to enjoy themselves. Has the park ever let down a dog who expects to go there and have fun? While animals have highlights that they remember and tell me about in a session, they don't compare one moment to the next in the way we do. They don't come away from the dog park saying, "Well, it was way more fun two days ago."

Secretariat was famous for standing in the corner for a few days if he didn't win a race, but then when he emerged from his stall for each new competition, it was a fresh opportunity. If he was in a race, it was *the* race. There wasn't any race before, and there wouldn't be another—this was it.

Oh, we have so much to learn from animals! Ultimately, we get a lot of soul growth because of them. Aren't we lucky!?

Before moving on, I want to acknowledge the first great famous animal communicator, St. Francis of Assisi. He actually conducted Mass for the birds! In his biography of St. Francis, Omer Englebert wrote:

> But no one in the West ever experienced or expressed as did St. Francis such a feeling of universal brotherhood of all creation. His heart is the way one pictures Adam's in the Garden of Eden; and it is to be believed that the very beasts perceived it, for they always showed such gratitude for the honor he paid them.

One day when out walking with friends, all the people around St. Francis noticed how many birds were filling the field. He told the people that he wanted to preach to them. He started out his sermon by saying: "My little sisters, the birds, many are the bonds that unite us to God."

After his bird Mass, he raised his hands up and the birds bowed to him. This worship, adoration, and love wasn't limited to birds. St. Francis took such great pleasure in all of God's creations that he was followed by animals everywhere. He also talked to the plants and flowers, and he was even known for walking reverently on stones.

177

✤ *Chapter Nine* ✤

RECEIVING FEELINGS, WORDS, AND PICTURES

I want to realize brotherhood or identity
not merely with the beings called human, but I want to realize iden-
tity with all life, even with such things as crawl upon the earth.
— Mahatma Gandhi

There are four principles that I try to live by. I'm not always successful, but since I first became aware of them, they've remained in the back of my mind. They are:

1. Always be of service (that is, give).
2. Always be full of gratitude.
3. Always forgive.
4. Always be available to receive.

They sound so simple. Of course, if you were operating at full tilt, living each of the four principles all the time, you could ascend into the ether! My early spiritual teacher and friend Susan Davis used to say that the most difficult principle for most of us is the last one: to receive.

We could give away the store. We might forget to be filled with gratitude but then go back to it. We could be working on forgiveness. But for some of us, it's hard to accept a compliment, let alone truly receive the abundance that's there for us. And it's no different in the microcosm of animal-communication work—it appears that it's harder to receive than to send.

Becoming a Receiver

People always ask if I hear another voice when I'm communicating with an animal. It's not as if a papillon dog sounds to me like some French dude, or that I actually hear speech. Rather, it's a different rhythm that comes from being aware of the landscape of my own being on a daily, moment-to-moment basis. Then I can become conscious when another voice, feeling, or physical sensation comes into my awareness.

It would be fun to think I was hearing some grande dame cat with a smoky Lauren Bacall voice, but in truth I'm not. When I say a "different rhythm," I mean that I'm aware of the way *my* mind thinks. I know when I'm in a great place and when I'm in a lofty, dreamy land. I'm aware of when I'm full of discontent. I know the fabric of my own mind. If I connect with myself and find that it's a great focus day (kind of like a good hair day) but then connect with an animal and suddenly feel as though the thoughts are all over the place, I know that the animal may very well have a concentration problem. I can start to get a sense of what it will take for the person to train the animal (particularly if it's young).

EVERYTHING IS ENERGY

Are you someone who shorts out electrical circuits? Are all animals drawn to you? We are little beacons of energy, sending and receiving at all times—and often we aren't even aware of what our energetic field is emitting. Frequently, it gets damaged before an illness enters our physical system. The imbalance has begun in our energy field before it shows up, say, in the form of blood work. Or if we're in an emotional state, we aren't aware of how much we're in our heads or our hearts, which also affects our field, creating an imbalance.

It's fun to think that our house is haunted or that a dead relative is visiting us. In truth, a lot of the quirky little things that happen around us are due to our own energy fields being out of balance. It's not always on account of so-called negative emotions. This can even be the case when we're super-excited about something: We can blow a fuse then, too. Taking a moment each day to pull all of your energy in and then let it back out is an excellent practice.

We're all little broadcasting machines, sending and receiving feelings, words, and pictures constantly. One of the biggest tools for becoming aware of what you're receiving is learning to turn off your internal chatter. Think of it like switching off your cell phone before watching a film in a movie theater. Another component is getting into a neutral state emotionally. The more you're a blank slate when doing this work, the better.

When you're available to listen to another being, what you *think* doesn't matter. Having a way of putting your own thoughts elsewhere temporarily is powerful for both you as the listener and the animal (or person) you're listening to. You can practice this as a friend or co-worker is telling you a story. Even in regular spoken communication, so many times your mind is distracted.

When you're truly listening to other beings, your *feelings* don't matter either: It's all about *them*. If you're in a particular emotional state, you're going to respond from that state. Having the ability to be in a neutral "nothing" place is desirable. For a few minutes a day, see if you can let your thoughts and feelings go like removing a cloak. Let them wash off in the shower. Allow them to be set aside as you get in your car and put the seat belt on. Permit them to be released when you have that first cup of tea or coffee. Some people have received pictures, words, and feelings from their animals just from being able to momentarily release the ongoing thoughts and feelings that swim around in their minds.

Meditation

For me, meditation is a very important component of this work, and I always start out by doing one in each of the classes that I teach. Some people meditate in a special physical location; others only go to a special place in their minds or hearts. Some individuals take walks or do exercises that are meditative, particularly rhythmic aerobic workouts (it's a perfect opportunity for saying prayers or mantras).

HOW TO MEDITATE

1. Start by sitting quietly and comfortably and becoming aware of your breath. Some people find it helpful to inhale to a count of 4 and exhale to a count of 8.

Become aware of any residual feelings clinging to you. Are you happy? Is life so good that you can't sit still and you feel the need to wriggle? Are you sad today? Are you tired? If so, are you exhausted by anything in particular—and are you willing to let that go? If you

HOW TO MEDITATE, CONT'D.

aren't able to do so permanently, can you at least let it go for now? Feelings come and go. Allow yourself to release them with a loud *Ahhh!* Shake them free with the vibration of the sound.

2. Next, examine your thoughts. Are they full of spam? Are you distracted? Are you clear? What's the landscape of your own mental patterns? You can even entertain a spam thought that's annoying—but only for a moment—then ask it to leave. Maybe it's something you want to come back to later, such as a forgiveness issue, or perhaps it should go on to your to-do list. It's a good idea to keep a pad of paper and a pen next to you as you quiet your mind so that the thought has a place to go since you don't need to review it now.

Again, if many thoughts are plaguing you, gently ask them to leave. Staying aware of your breath is important. When you feel as though you're ready to have an empty space between your ears, let out another big *Ahhh!* and allow the vibration of the sound to unhook all of those thoughts.

3. The third place to observe awareness is in your body. Where is your physical tension today, this minute? Did you wake up sore? Do you have aches and pains? Are you feeling tired? Are you at your usual energy level?

Now for a moment draw your attention up through your whole body: How do your toes feel today? How about your feet? Work your way higher through your legs, your torso, and all your organs and glands. How is your chest? What about your heart and lungs? Continue on up to your shoulders, your arms, and your fingers. Check your neck and backbone. How is your whole head (even your hair)? How are your senses today—dull, clear, available? Again, let out the little niggling physical tensions with a big *Ahhh!*

4. Now assess the whole again and see if anything else is pressing. If so, ask it to leave for the moment. If not, then continue on, maintaining your awareness of your breathing. Once your mind is clear, connecting up with One Mind is as simple as concentrating on your breath.

When connecting with animals, you may find it easier at first if they're quietly sitting next to you in the room. But this doesn't always work out: Sometimes the intense focus alone forces them to do something cute! The animal may be eating, or be running around and playing. We humans can be engaged in activities and still communicate (yes, I've been known to think while chewing and even, God forbid, to speak with my mouth full), and so can they.

It's okay if there are other pets in the room as long as you're able to connect with the one you want to communicate with. If you're having trouble doing so, create a white light bridge between its heart and yours. Or imagine that you're surrounding that animal with pink and are connected to this pink bubble. You could also merge your field with that of the animal, creating a space (One Mind) for it to safely communicate in.

The One Mind concept is a great reminder that we *are* all one, and it's a great place just to practice some basics of learning to receive feelings.

Start by being aware of all that you are. Become aware of your breath for a moment and then of your entire being. Start from the very center of your body, between your heart and your solar plexus, and imagine it to be the core of your very being. On an exhale, see how far that being extends. You'll start to get a sense of your entire field of energy, what's called the auric field. *Take a moment and breathe in all that is you . . . and breathe out all that is you. As a next step, imagine that you're inhaling love . . . and exhaling love.*

Your animal companion also has a surrounding field. Close your eyes and imagine that you're sensing its size. Now imagine that the two fields—yours and your animal's—are merging. As you exhale, send the animal love and see what comes back in the form of breath: Are you being sent love? Anxiety? Contentedness? Anger? You don't want to hang on to the feelings, so consciously release them, again exhaling and transmitting love.

When this exercise feels complete, thank the animal for the exchange. Take a moment to acknowledge your pet as a unique being who's part of your whole experience, at the same time recognizing yourself as being unique and a part of your animal's experience.

You don't have to sit around to do this exercise. If you have a dog who loves to play catch, go outside, merge your fields, and then see what feelings come and go as you toss the ball. Try it before playing with a toy that makes your cat go crazy in a fun way. The joy that gets passed back and forth is awesome. This is also an excellent exercise to do before riding.

Additionally, you can practice sending in a bigger way so that your animal companions get an even more profound sense of the pleasure you receive from working together with them, and you can send that back in the form of gratitude. This is truly an awe-inspiring exercise, especially for the animal who's been a challenge in training, perhaps one you've exhibited a fair amount of frustration with. Here's a little opportunity to sink into One Mind for that moment the animal is in tune with you, letting it know, without words, just how much you do love it.

Forging a Connection

If you are doing this for a friend, you may or may not want the person to be in the room with you. I personally prefer the animal's guardian to be present, as I may have questions during the session. Your friend may also have questions and can ask them before or after you first tune in to the animal.

Initially, I want to use that deeply connected moment to gather as much information as I can before I speak out loud to the person. Everyone is different, so you may find it easier to tell your friend what the animal is communicating to you as you're going along. The main reason why I don't go about it in that way is because I want to experience the whole free-form flow of the animal's communication with me. This gives me an idea of how it thinks, how it perceives things, and what's at the root of its behavior. Once I start speaking out loud, the other person usually has a thousand questions. Suddenly there's an agenda or a theme around a specific issue and then we may never get to the root of the problem.

I always write down the impressions I get, since there's often so much information coming at me that I don't want to forget some key point that could unlock a situation for the person. I then do a question-and-answer session after my initial connection with the animal.

Once you've used meditation to help you focus on receiving, bring the animal you want to communicate with into your awareness. Some people like to bring it into their heart; others prefer bringing it into their mind's eye (the third eye). Sometimes right before I connect, I'll shut my eyes just to close out the rest of the world for a minute. When a situation in my own life is challenging,

I keep my eyes closed for most of the reading, but I know how to "get there"—to that void—pretty quickly . . . it becomes habitual with practice. Still, even for me, some days are harder than others.

Begin the connection by asking if it's okay to communicate with the animal(s). You may feel an opening up or sense relief from them because they've been waiting for this. You could simply "hear" a yes, which will have a different texture from your usual thoughts, as though someone else literally placed the word in your brain. Usually the animal will sense that it's safe to connect with you because your intention is pure. Being quiet and sitting for a moment to tune in to yourself first is a great way to ensure that safety.

If it's your own animal companion and you have a simple question, go ahead and ask it and see what floats into your head. As you keep practicing simple questions, see how quickly words, thoughts, and feelings come in. Frequently the first thing—or few things—is the animal's true reply.

If it's a new animal or a friend's, start by asking it about its favorite things, such as toys, activities, and treats. By doing so, you're familiarizing yourself with the animal and making it receptive to more important questions. Familiarity also brings in a sense of the animal's essence—who it is in the world and how it sees itself. You can ask the animal how it feels about its situation in general: What is its emotional state?

Next you can try to get a sense of the animal's relationships. How is its connection with the human members of the household? How does it get along with the other pets who live there? How does it feel when it meets new animals or people?

What is its physical state like? Is the animal tired, or is it frisky? Does it have sufficient opportunity to express itself physically? Is it in pain? Does it feel slowed down in any particular part of its body?

Some of the answers will bring up more questions. You can also ask if there's anything that it wants to share. Once you feel complete, thank the animal.

The information is worth writing down, as it comes in fast and sometimes it's nonsensical. Spend too much time over any one point and you end up feeling as though you should guess at everything. It's as if there's a pop quiz in algebra that you forgot to study for and you won't get to go to lunch if you don't at least make something up. Know that your imagination plays a role in this, so just be aware of the images or words that come up.

Telepathic communication is surprisingly simple, and there are times when these questions may seem *too* straightforward. Once you can ask basic questions and get a response that you can either verify by your animal's behavior or that makes you look at something from a different angle, you've built up your telepathic muscle. After that, of course, you can get more specific.

Anchoring the Good Feelings

If you're working with your own animal and you want to really have an impact on a challenging situation, go back in your own mind to a time when you had the sensation of a perfect moment. Let's say that you have a cat who has trouble getting along with other felines in the household; however, that cat can sit in your lap and send you love through a purr like nobody else. Close your eyes and imagine the sensation of that peaceful purring in your lap. Anchor that sensation into your being for a few moments.

Now maintain that sensation as you merge your field with that of the cat for a moment, and continue to breathe in and out. Take a few moments to anchor in that feeling for the cat. Now slowly but surely, allow that sensation to expand in both of your fields. When it has grown to include both of you and the love is nearly overwhelming, in your mind's eye imagine the other animals entering the merged field. Now sit with the sensation of all these animals together in this field of bliss.

I have many enlightened rides with my horse Rollie. Then if I'm having a bad day on the road, I like to anchor in that feeling of our unity when we're riding just to get through bad traffic! (And no, I don't close my eyes while I'm driving!) I just allow that sensation to fill my entire being, expand it to my field, and allow it out. Usually other drivers stay out of my way.

Anchoring in sensations could be something you do even while you're grooming your horse. It's also good before a basic obedience class with a new puppy. Recollect whatever moment was absolutely perfect, merge the fields, and sit with it for a moment; then expand it out for both you and the animal to feel. Start to pull things that are a challenge for both of you into the field in your mind's eye, yet hold strong to the excellent feeling that you're experiencing together in the merging.

Guidelines for Connecting with Others

Often when people take one of my classes, they realize that they connect more easily with someone else's animal than they do with their own. The reason for this is very simple: People don't have an agenda with someone else's animal.

Of course you want your cat to tell you that red is her favorite color if you've just invested in a ruby collar. If *you* like trail riding, you want your horse to agree. Like all of us, you wish your dog would tell you that it's okay that you're a workaholic. You want to hear the bird say that he won't bite your niece's fingers when she pokes at him.

Other students of mine are afraid that they'll hear that their animal doesn't love them. That fear and the resulting hesitation blocks the process. First and foremost, animals are way more forgiving than we humans are. Perhaps things could be better between you, but the love is there or you wouldn't have been motivated to pick up this book in the first place. Maybe the animal is going through the same issues or challenges that you are with respect to showing affection or expressing love—or worse, is struggling to find the connection with you. But love is always there. Start the communication process from a place of caring.

If you're doing this for a friend, even the simplest image you receive is so exciting. If you feel comfortable enough to express it to your friend and he or she is able to confirm the truth of the image, it helps you know that you're on the right track. If you're able to telepathically receive a very simple piece of information, such as the animal's favorite activity or food, ask your friend if this is correct. Keep this up as you go along, just for your own clarification. It's the little things about the animal that add up to the whole communication picture.

A word of caution about communicating with a friend's animal: Make sure that you're doing this for someone who's supportive. In the beginning, negative attitudes toward this work can be a true buzz kill! You need the emotional safety, the support, and the space in which to engage in another's world.

There are three other things that I stress in my classes:

1. Diplomacy
2. Ethics
3. Neutrality

Diplomacy

Diplomacy is very important when you're the interpreter. If a dog is acting out about a situation, I can't take on the animal's frustration when I convey this to the human. If I start at that level, the person is going to get defensive and shut down, or worse, the situation could escalate. In either case, the guardian can become less likely to take measures to alleviate the unwanted behavior.

Ultimately, I'm really not serving the animal by taking sides. Being self-aware by recognizing my own emotional triggers and staying neutral are key components of diplomacy. If appropriate, humor can lighten up many situations. Laughter, like tears, is a form of release, after which you can get to the heart of the matter. Being available to *everyone* concerned is part of being an animal communicator.

Ethics

Ethics is vital to this area of work. If I'm invited over to your house for dinner, I don't come in and talk to your animal—I come as a guest. If I'm invited over to your house to talk to your cat, *then* I'll talk to the cat.

It's also not okay for me to tell tales out of school about the quality of the relationship between an animal and its person. If someone asks me how a session went, I stick to the cute things—the horse loves to jump, for instance, or the dog wants to go on more car rides. Beyond that, "What happens in Vegas, stays in Vegas." It's up to the animal's guardian to share the more intimate details with friends.

Acting ethically is important when you start connecting on a deeper level. It's not all right to tune in to the neighbor's dog because you *assume* that things are going badly or that the animal is being mistreated. This form of communication should be used with discretion, with permission, and with the best of intentions.

In one of my classes, a woman told a story about how she saw a dog tied to a tree. Horrified, she "saved" the animal by taking him home. A little later that day, the police came to her door to arrest her for stealing the dog. He'd been tied to the tree next to a school while a young mother was picking up her daughters. The dog wasn't allowed on school property but loved the kids and lived to pick them up each day.

You have to understand the contractual agreement between animals, their guardians, and God. It's a journey with the Divine and their souls. What might look horrible to you and me may in fact be a very healing experience *for them*. Even if someone does ask for help, you can't be committed or attached to the outcome. Yes, at times I speak passionately, but once I leave that household or barn, I pray for the highest good of all involved—but I can't begin to know *what* that is. It's spiritual arrogance to think that we know better than God. Animal communication doesn't "solve" anything; it just creates an opportunity for the person and the pet to shift out of the locked emotions, negative behavior, or illness and get back on track.

I say this because many professions have a code of honor, an association, or rules to live by. While not everyone follows them, it's important to know the guidelines. The more objective and compassionate you remain, the greater the opportunity for healing. There's always a set of bylaws inherent in a pack, a herd, a pride, or a flock . . . all have their own natural order. Whether this is something that you intend to do for your life's work or just to help your friends out, it still requires that you maintain certain personal and professional boundaries—like any other job.

Neutrality

Leave as neutral as you came: Self-awareness and being unbiased are as important coming out of the communication as they were going in. You don't want to take on the emotions, illness, and behavior of the animal or humans involved. Certainly nobody would like to see you take up barking when the neighborhood dogs pass by!

Seriously, you can't afford to absorb any of it, and doing so wouldn't be helping anyone. It's detrimental to you, and if you're knocked down by someone else's "stuff," that's one less animal or person you're helping.

Frequently I'll ask students in a class if they ever carry a low-grade depression. Many folks will raise their hands. Then I inquire, "Are you sure that it's yours?" meaning that we're all absorbing so much *stuff* into our psyches, our hearts, and our subconscious.

Unless you're a complete narcissist or sociopath, you're empathic. Awareness, which has been discussed throughout this chapter, is helpful here, too. Something as simple as using concentrated breathing to become centered can assist you in clearing yourself. Just take a moment to exhale all that's not yours. On the inhale, breathe in love. You even can do several breaths like this in the car before you start your ignition or when you get off the phone after an unpleasant conversation. It's a powerful technique in life.

Another technique is to literally shake it off for three minutes. Getting in the shower and imagining you're washing off the emotional soot of the day helps as well. In addition, aerobic exercise allows you to clear away the cobwebs that stick to you from other people and animals. If you aren't going to start spinning classes tomorrow at the local gym, at least take a stroll down your street.

Family and Friends

I discussed earlier that doing this work with emotional safety is the best way to start. You don't need other people's opinions to make you back down from your dream of communicating freely with your own animals and others. You always have to remember that everyone acts with free will.

My Dad and Chase

This lesson was brought home to me in an unexpected way recently. My father is proud of my work and what I've done. At first he wasn't quite sure what it was, but then in the late '90s when I ended up on TV as an animal communicator, he claimed that I got the gift from *his* side of the family! I used to explain time and again that this isn't a gift, that we're all animal communicators. I let him know that even *he* was one.

My father is 87 years old. We lost my mother in September of 2004, and my dad is a fabulous character in his own right, but let's face it—my mom did a lot. My father still practices law and loves working. Recently, though, some of his physical conditions caught up with him. Usually my father can "buck up," so to speak, but this time he had pneumonia as well as other complications, and it scared him.

Then his dog, Chase, was diagnosed with cancer (truly she was originally my mother's best friend). My father informed me that if the vet told him to put the dog down, he was going to do it. He also spoke of his own mortality in a frightening tone. It broke my heart to think of them both leaving the planet soon. I offered to take Chase, but my dad was firm that he would follow the vet's orders.

I didn't hear from him for a day or so after that, and then when I finally did talk to him, my dad said, "Joan,

I've made a decision." I braced myself. "I'm broken down and Chase is broken down, and I've decided that I don't care what the vet says. When I look in her eyes, she's still alive. She doesn't want to commit suicide, so we'll just hobble around and struggle together."

The day my dad realized what the dog was communicating to him was a lucky one. As much as I was ready to fly in and pick Chase up or have a friend do so, I had to step back and trust that my dad was able to make a decision that wasn't based on his fear of his own mortality in that moment.

The people closest to us can make decisions or do things that would hurt us more than a complete stranger making the same decision or taking the same course of action. So stepping outside ourselves and staying in One Mind, holding strong to the belief that the other person is able to make the right choice, is an important lesson.

Connecting with the "Other Side"

Whether you believe in the afterlife or past lives—or neither—look again at the concept I brought up in Chapter 1 of "stickiness" between beings. As I mentioned, quantum physics says that anytime two things are brought together and then taken apart, a stickiness occurs. Think of that sticky content as a great recorder of all that is. When you go into One Mind, it becomes available to you.

A great thing that you can do to ease your mind when a pet has crossed over is to center yourself in One Mind, breathe in love, and merge fields with that animal companion. As you're sending caring feelings out, make space for the love that will come back in waves.

This can be a profound way of releasing your own guilt over any decisions you felt awkward about making toward the end of the animal's life. It also can help you accept the outcome and understand that the love is always there and may act as counsel in your life, guiding you to make decisions from the heart rather than the mind. While your companion is no longer in physical form, perhaps through this exercise you'll see the abundance of love and guidance that is still available to you. And you may have an opportunity to see that there is no "other" side . . . it's all one.

I don't spend an enormous amount of time on this subject in my animal-communication classes, partly because I'm helping people truly build that telepathic muscle. Usually, seeing people go from picking up on one or two tangible things to receiving whole paragraphs is exciting enough. I want to anchor in that experience strongly before advancing to something that's less verifiable (especially since people have to go home and try it without the safety net of the group and the guidance of a teacher).

❖ Chapter Ten ❖

OVERALL WELLNESS

*The purity of a person's heart can be quickly measured by how they
regard animals.*
— Anonymous

The importance of paying attention to overall wellness to me is just basic. With all the information out
there for us humans to better understand how to use our
own energy more effectively, there's also that much data
available about animals.

There are certain ways we fed horses as recently as
the 1970s that are now known to be counterproductive.
There are overprocessed commercial pet foods that are
really downright dangerous for the health of our animal
companions. I would consider assessing nutrition to be
the biggest tool I use when trying to sort out the behavior
and ascertain the well-being of an animal.

Become aware of the following:

- What are your animals eating?
- Is that food serving them in the best way it can?
- Do your animals have energy?
- Are they cranky?

If *you* had gotten a vaccination, stopped at the store for a doughnut, picked up a fast-food hamburger on the way home, and had a few cupcakes for dinner (not to mention supplemented your day with gallons of coffee) . . . how do you think *you* would feel after all that? Would *you* be nice to anyone? Would *you* respond heroically to a boss's demands? Wouldn't you want to curl up in bed?

I'm putting these ridiculous questions here because that pretty much amounts to what most people are unknowingly doing to their animals as a result of what they're feeding them.

Nutrition

I've been studying this subject for years. I'll review some basics and then lead you to some other resources. Suffice it to say, I'm passionate about the food issue. This is partly because I know the mistakes *I* made with the two horses I lost in the early 1990s. Yes, their time was their time. However, with what I know now, it would have certainly been a different fight. I also grew up with a dog who lived to be 23 years old, and I thought that was normal. Now I see so many animals die at such young ages, and I believe that the early seeds of illness can be traced back to the preservatives in many commercial foods and other toxins in the environment. The pet-food industry is getting hip to this, but not fast enough.

The Law of Attraction states: "Like attracts like." If you're feeding your animals frequency-raising meals—meaning minerals, herbs, and organic foods—you're automatically pulling in better energy for them. If you're exposing your animals to energy killers such as daily wormers, pesticides and herbicides (on food and grass), antibiotics, chlorinated water, preservatives, and mercury (in vaccines), you're automatically bringing down the vibration. These are things to be mindful of. The body is a natural responder to "like attracts like."

In *The Non-Toxic Farming Handbook,* Philip A. Wheeler, Ph.D., and Ronald B. Ward state:

> Fertilizers also serve to attract similar nutrients to themselves. The nutrient energies being attracted in the soil are carried over the surface of the earth on the same magnetic currents that operate a compass. To maximize the attraction of energies, the farmer must consciously plan to create as broad a "magnetic base" as possible. Raising organic (humus) levels, balancing calcium, magnesium and phosphate levels is required here. This creates a highly beneficial environment for soil microbes which will add to soil fertility.
>
> A fertile soil in good tilth will continue to grow more fertile because the balance of nutrient energies serves to attract balanced energies in return. This works in the opposite as well. By adding the toxic energies with "kill" frequencies to the soil, the soil will attract similar energies to it. As the soil becomes more and more out of balance, it will attract an imbalance of energies to it. The rich get richer, the poor get poorer.

Food as Fuel

One of the biggest energy tools of all time and for all beings is food. You are what you eat, as the saying goes. Yet the quality of food we expect our animals to ingest and still be healthy equates to putting Mountain Dew in our gas tank and expecting to be able to drive across the state. To start with, our land has been worked over; the earth is now deficient in mineral content—which is the life force of the planet. Add to that the fact that the environment is pesticide filled, so we're further killing off the land's life force. Then the pet-food industry puts all sorts of absurd preservatives in their bagged and canned food.

Think about how you feel after eating less-than-great food. But perhaps that's a habit for you and you're used to low levels of energy or less-than-perfect health. It's all a choice, right? Because we tend to feed the same thing over and over to our animals, we aren't offering *them* that same choice.

Finding out what will serve your animal's immune system best is invaluable to their well-being. Being responsible for your pets isn't just a matter of getting them out for exercise and caring for their emotional needs. It's also about letting the day start out as great as it can by giving them the best nutrition.

How can we expect them to *behave well* when we're feeding them the equivalent of a cheeseburger with fries? How can we expect them to *perform well* when we're giving them sugary doughnuts? How can we expect them to *get well* when we feed them poorly?

It used to be that inbreeding caused some degenerative diseases and, in some cases, could produce an almost "possessed" form of behavior. Now the average mix-breed animal has its own problems, suffering from the legacy of generations of junk-food diets and over-vaccination. These beings are coming onto a planet that is deficient, and our feeding ideas are only making things worse for them.

As if it's not enough that our animals are exposed to toxins just by going on the neighbor's pesticide-covered lawn or being near the chemical carpet cleaners we're using, they're also certainly getting heavy metals in the pesticides used on the vegetables that are in their food.

Always look for organic food. When a label says "natural," that word doesn't really have any scientific meaning and may be just something that the marketing director told them to put there. So you should really dig and learn how to read labels. On my Website, I've posted information on how to do so. If nothing else, it's important that you don't see the following ingredients:

- BHT
- BHA
- Ethoxoquin

BHA and BHT are known carcinogens. They're almost entirely out of the foods that humans consume, although some may contain traces of them. Even if you were to consume one of these ingredients in a bowl of processed cereal one morning, you still might eat a variety of healthier foods that day. Meanwhile, we feed the same thing over and over to our dogs and cats, thereby exposing them to high levels of carcinogens. Ethoxoquin is a product that's used to preserve rubber in tires. So while it's excellent for our automobiles—you guessed it—it's bad for the animals.

The next label lesson is: *by-products*. Many of the things that appear to be meat are actually meat by-products—nonmeat animal parts such as feet, beaks, and a whole host of other things that are well described in the book *Food Pets Die For* by Ann N. Martin.

Food is energy, and we know that St. Francis of Assisi revered the earth and all of its offerings. How could we then not feed our beautiful friends the perfection that's offered here? We really should begin with the soil so that we're creating a better starting point for all food products.

Buffet-Style

The problem isn't just what we feed our animals, but *how* we feed them. Out in the wild, no dog or cat ever had a free-choice buffet-style diet for an easy-dining experience. Leaving food out all day may be convenient for you so that you don't worry about the animal getting enough, but it's not necessarily best for them. You can easily retrain animals' eating habits. Some people believe one meal is enough, but others believe in two a day.

Animals' digestive tract and enzymes are connected to the process of eating when hungry. Since dogs and cats are predators in the wild—meat eaters—this also involves a hunt. In modern times, occasionally they get lucky and dinner comes in the form of roadkill, but they had to have been trotting along for a while before they stumbled upon that. Something else might have smelled it also, so they have to watch as they eat and be ready to skedaddle if a bigger predator comes along.

Many clients have heard me tell them to play "Serengeti" with their cats—that is, mimic the conditions cats

would face in the wild by finding the right toys (specifically ones they can chase) and getting them to play with
each other . . . whatever it takes. As I mentioned, I get
my dog and cat playing together right before a meal, and
now I don't even have to participate—it has become a
habit. For cats, it could involve a little crouching down,
jumping, and running before you let them feast . . . then
they've earned it! For dogs, just get them out to play
and run (toss the ball around for them while you have
that first cup of coffee or tea) before you put their food
down.

Years ago I was teaching for a weekend in Lawrence,
Kansas. I met a wonderful woman who had a sanctuary
for birds of prey. She had built this immense cage for an
injured hawk that gave it room to fly a bit without exac-
erbating its injury. The reason she called me out was that
this wonderful hawk started attacking her when she came
in to feed it—and only did so at these times. The woman
was distraught; this hawk had always shown her such
love and appreciation. When I tuned in to the animal, it
shared its appreciation for, and devotion to, the woman.
However, there was an underlying tension around the
food.

I told the woman, "Look, you can take an animal out
of the wild, but you can't take the wild out of the animal.
You're doing what you can with the best of intentions,
and the hawk knows that she wouldn't survive in the
wild. But at feeding time she's associating you with the
food, and she's missing that 'wild thing' that hawks do." I
couldn't explain what that "wild thing" was because, God
knows, if it were up to me to catch and kill my dinner, I'd
be eating grass. I suggested that she throw the food into
the big cage with untamed abandon; that way the hawk

could swoop down on it, fulfilling that wild thing, and their loving relationship would be maintained.

Not only did this work, but the woman really enjoyed being part of that world. She created elaborate ways of allowing the hawk to express its instincts, while maintaining safety for both human and bird.

Horses are the exception to the no-buffet rule. Plant eaters by nature, horses move and eat at all times, so when they're stalled, make sure that there's always hay in front of them. Be a nuisance to your barn manager, pay the groom extra—do whatever it takes to make sure that the horse's gut is active at all times. And remember this: "At all times" really, truly means *at all times*.

When communicating with horses, I always ask the owners what breed they are. If the horse falls into a certain category, I automatically ask if it's imported. When the horse has come from Europe, the first place I go is the stomach. Europeans feed horses much differently from the way North Americans do, so there's quite a change when they get food products here. As a result, many imported horses have a tendency to colic.

We live in a society where obesity is a major problem. We're also creating this crisis in our pets. Now animals are not only suffering from the same ghastly cancers that humans do, but also from insulin resistance and thyroid problems. (Can you imagine?)

These health issues not only hinder an animal's wellness but also inhibit good behavior. Before I even check to see what could have happened in a dog's life to make it aggressive, I look over the thyroid and the cranial bones. Problems with either could give the dog a headache. If it's a blood-sugar condition, the headache is the least of it—no one would "be nice" in that condition.

As Nature Intended

The very best way for animals to eat, of course, is the way nature intended. However, since we can't create hunting grounds out of our backyards or at the dog park, finding healthy food is a place to start. Always read labels, select an organic pet food, and consider supplementing it with raw food—and I don't mean pizza crust.

Some people have fears about feeding animals raw foods. If you choose to do so, there are several books listed in the Resources section that have excellent recipes. Also, there are reputable raw-food companies out there that take the guesswork out of it for you (you'll find the Websites for them, too).

Raw food isn't for everyone. Some animals can't handle it because of prior feeding regimens, toxins in their system, and so on. Many people, though, wouldn't feed their animals anything *but* raw food. However, you should always supplement it. Even the best raw-food diet needs a little vitamin-and-mineral boost.

A lot of people say, "Aren't you afraid to give your dog raw meat, with all that bacteria?" For one thing, a dog is willing to eat days-old roadkill, then just trot off looking for the next big adventure! The other reason I feel okay about it is that canine digestive tracts are short and can handle the bacteria because it passes through quickly. Their enzymes are sitting in there, waiting to break it down.

I personally feed my dog and cat the tiniest amount of kibble (coarsely ground meal or grain) in the morning to make them think that they're getting breakfast. I usually put a raw egg on it, which is so exciting to them that if there's something that I have to get into them (such as a strong-tasting omega-3 capsule or herbal parasite control), I can hide it in there. They also get raw meat at night. I switch the meats around weekly, using organic chicken, red meat, and turkey—including bones and organs. This is combined with a mix of raw organic vegetables—for example, broccoli, asparagus, potato, and carrots. I like a mix of several root veggies with several above-ground ones. I blend this in advance and keep it in the refrigerator for a few days.

Some people question why I feed vegetables to my dog and cat. If you were to look at the stomach contents of a predator, you would find vegetation. Not only that, but the prey that they eat is full of it. Oftentimes, the first place predators will go is the stomach of their prey. We've all seen a dog or cat go out and eat grass—this is their version of Tums.

My cat gets ¼ cup of meat and a heaping tablespoon of the veggie mix. For the dog, I do 1½ cups of meat and 3 heaping tablespoons of the veggie mix. I also include a probiotic (a supplement of "good" bacteria that aids digestion), a combination vitamin/mineral supplement, an herbal-green formula, additional vitamin C, and omega-3 fatty acids. Throughout the year, I do herbal parasite and heavy-metal cleanses (as a result of any exposure to pesticides or other toxins around the house—and yes, everyone has toxins in their home).

When I was having behavior issues with my horse Rollie, I changed his feed to "cool his jets." I took him off a "senior feed" that's full of preservatives and put him on a slightly modified organic corn, oats, and barley (C.O.B.) grain by Dynamite, which is the only chemical-free feed mill in the country. (Because of that fact, I've become a distributor for their foods—please visit my Website for more information.) Dynamite also offers superb organic products for animals, including supplements with amino-acid-chelated minerals. Not all vitamins and minerals are the same. Finding products that contain amino-acid chelates is important because that means they're already bio-available for the system; otherwise, a lot of times they'll just go out in the urine and not be absorbed by the body.

The Importance of pH Balance

The noted wellness expert Dr. Andrew Weil suggests that the stomach is actually the second brain. Digestive issues can be at the root of so many behavioral issues. Nearly every illness can be linked to the stomach. Look at how our animals react to barometric-pressure changes: Their stomachs feel the effects long before the storm comes in.

The pH (that is, the balance of acidity and alkalinity) of the body's system is everything when it comes to maintaining good health. The abbreviation *pH* stands for "potential of hydrogen." Learning about pH and how to balance it—whether it's in the stomach, the blood, the urine, or our soils—will not only help your animal companion, but may enlighten you to make changes in your own system as well. It's all about balance. Think in terms of trying to get this "second brain" running right.

Acid/alkaline balance controls the bacterial content of the body. It also affects mood, performance, mental functions, behavior, and even skeletal structure. Blood pH has to be alkaline, but when we use our muscles, we produce acid. Someone I share many clients with, Regan Golob, D.C., (who works on humans and animals) says,

Basically our system is alkaline by design and acid by function. People need to understand what creates acid: emotional stress creates acid, environmental stress creates acid, vaccines create acid. Anything you introduce foreign to the system creates an acid residue. Then you need to use alkaline minerals to buffer it and remove it from the system.

Learning which foods create alkalinity in the system helps. For example, the darker the green vegetable is, usually the higher the alkalinity. (Don't just use that as your rule of thumb, though—find an alkaline/acid chart. I have one on my Website.)

Vaccines

Vaccination is a controversial subject. The damage done from a vaccine reaction can be far worse than the disease itself, so another option is to learn to manage the animal's immune system. I've seen many neurological tragedies or brutal cancers from over-vaccination. If your pet isn't exposed to many other animals, you may decide against vaccination. Educate yourself and choose from your heart. Sometimes vaccines are automatically given "just because."

I honor any choice people make. The first step, though, is accepting that it *is* a choice. If you do feel the need to vaccinate or it's required for showing, traveling, or boarding your animals, treat them to some immune-building supplements to counter the fallout. You can also get titer tests at your vet's office, which actually show the level of antibodies from a vaccine that's still present in the system. This creates a baseline to operate from, rather than simply saying, "Ready, aim, vaccinate." If you're showing your animals or taking them to doggy day care, be mindful of what's truly needed. Again, the best defense is a healthy immune system.

Getting blood work done to see what your animal is facing isn't a bad idea. Try not to have the annual visit to the veterinarian just be about a vaccine. Many vets are learning about the tragic results of over-vaccination— such as tumors at the spot where the injection occurred or other types of cancer in the body—and new protocols are being established.

A Note on Training

In addition to seeing to it that your pet is physically healthy, you should be sure that training isn't necessary. This word comes up frequently in my sessions, even those involving a cat or a bird. Sometimes training just means spending the next six weeks being more conscious of who's in charge of the household, becoming the team manager instead of watching one of the other beings run things.

Having been a horse person most of my life, I know the value of training. When you're dealing with a 1,000-pound animal, it can be downright dangerous without training, boundaries, or respect. It's a matter of safety and security for dogs, cats, and birds as well.

People often argue that they don't want to break the animal's spirit—that logic would fall within the lines of what trainers call *loving a pet to death*. Some of us are fortunate because the dog or cat picks up on subtle cues or learns a command after the first time hearing it, but other animals may need a little more prodding. That nudge can come by way of creating better habits around situations, thus fostering safety.

Much behavior has its origins in survival. When animals moved into our households, however, behavior splintered off into being driven by the need for approval or control. You can watch your animals and see if the motive behind their actions fall into those three categories: survival/security, approval, or control. Some days the reason shifts. Anxiety around a thunderstorm, for example, begs for a form of safety. If you know that your animals react to the noise of fireworks on July 4, take extra measures to ensure their security *before* they get neurotic. In the same sense, if you know that your animal functions from the need for approval or control, by taking small steps in training you can still give it self-esteem or teach it to be a team player.

To me, training is just the foundation that you play or experiment with every day. It's like setting up a secret language that is unique to each animal yet at the same time enables everyone to play by the same rules. My dog is half border collie—a breed that's a full-time dog. When I'm not paying attention and not tuned in, she's like Wile E. Coyote. She gets a look in her eyes that's clearly blowing me off. We have to go back to boot camp when this happens. She has trained *me* so that rather than taking all of her rights away, I should be ahead of the game and do a little work with her every day.

I take learning and training seriously for animal communication. I've learned many modalities just so that I know the nature of the benefits of different healing techniques and can specifically recommend them. In particular, I can't get enough of training—it's something to put your trust in. There's as much in it for us as there is for the animals.

Your *Personal Habits*

I didn't always know how to communicate with animals. As I've already mentioned, I learned. But prior to taking animal-communication classes, I'd been meditating since I was about 24 and doing yoga on and off since my teens. I'd also taken plenty of energy-work classes.

This all came in very handy when I focused on being an animal communicator. Mind you, I never in ten million years thought that this would be my life's work; I was doing it for fun and to check in with my horse Gabrielle. I didn't realize that some of my habits were beneficial on the job.

Six days a week I start my day out with what I call the "hour of power." I exercise, and even if there's disco music on or I'm taking in the sights and sounds where I'm jogging/walking, I say prayers and affirmations while doing so. I also do yoga, ride several days a week, and try to sneak in at least one meditation a day.

One of the reasons why I advocate aerobic exercise is that those of us in this work—the very empathic or very smart types—live from about the fourth chakra (that is, the heart center) up. It's extremely important to stay grounded with this work. Aerobic exercise and yoga have the ability not only to ground you physically, but also to lessen the intensity of your thoughts and feelings.

I personally think of aerobic exercise as a natural Prozac! The rhythmic aspect of it becomes meditative—it's a good way just to get anchored in your body. It's really important to do so even if you don't feel as though you're sending or receiving information, since so many of us are empathic without realizing it. Not everybody likes to sit for meditation, but it doesn't have to be in a sitting pose. In addition, you can do *everything* in a meditative state.

After my physical routine, I write in a journal, trying to stay in observer mode instead of obsessing over a thought, feeling, or emotion that has a hook in me. Of course there are days when I ramble on, but other times I'm in observer mode before the pen touches the paper. When that's the case, I've already hit neutral, meaning that I'm not whining incessantly about something that has gone wrong or my feelings about what someone did to me. I find that if I'm not "aware" in the morning, I could easily fall into victim-of-my-own-life mode, and then the whole day goes that way.

On days I don't have time to write, I just do a quick mental check-in. Between the exercise and the writing, I'm pretty aware of how my mental, physical, emotional, and spiritual self is humming for the day, and I can make adjustments. I may not get mascara on before I leave the house, but I *will* tune my frequency as high as it can go for that day, given whatever I'm processing mentally or emotionally.

Some days my focus is excellent; on others you'd think I had a Twinkie hangover. When I glimpse the nature of my own state of being (every day is a snapshot in time), I can then see what I need to be aware of in order to be there for myself, my own animals, my clients, and my students. I can gauge how much work I have to do in order to get neutral.

Not everybody is going to go to the extremes that I do. I understand that, but it's important to have awareness of the world around you and what affects you—what triggers you—in order to be very available, not only for your own animals, but also for yourself.

I see (or connect with) so many animals on a weekly or daily basis, and with them comes a variety of dramas or illnesses that need to be addressed. I have to go the extra mile each day so that I'm ready to do so, as well as to make sure I'm not bringing my work home with me. Once in a while, of course, something will deeply affect me, and then I have to look at why this happens and ask myself, *What is this representing for me?*

❖ *Chapter Eleven* ❖

ENERGETIC SYSTEMS

God is really only another artist.
He invented the giraffe, the elephant,
and the cat. He has no real style. He
just keeps on trying other things.
— Pablo Picasso

The world is made up of energy. Scientists have broken it down into micro-units and examined it on a piece-by-piece basis. Yet, more and more we're recognizing that it's all part of a vast whole . . . and whether you call it an ecosystem or One Mind, we're all part of it.

We love maps or diagrams—we like to know which way to go. It's certainly easier to have a road atlas and know in advance how to get from New York to South Carolina rather than just getting in your car and guessing where the state is. Having maps to our energetic system is another wonderful way to begin to really read the situation at hand and identify the necessary tools to rectify it.

Behavior problems and illness have one thing in common: They've created a repatterning of the natural flow of energy. Long before there was blood work to see the blueprint of our inner workings, there were other "maps" to the body's energy system that healers have used.

One of those is the meridian system in Chinese medicine. *Meridians* are literally lines that flow through the body. Each one is associated with a different organ, which in turn is associated with a particular emotion. An acupuncturist will use the meridians to understand the system and see where the blocks in the energy flow are.

Coming from certain religious traditions of Asia (namely, Tibetan Buddhism and Hinduism), the chakras are another map to this system. *Chakra* is a Sanskrit word that means "wheel" or "circle." Each one is associated with particular mental, emotional, physical, and spiritual conditions and is linked to a specific color. Chakras also align with glands in the endocrine system, and there's a correspondence between them and the spine's connection with neurological centers. Chakras have been modernized through the New Age movement, and having even a slight understanding of them has become a standard for most energy workers.

UNDERSTANDING CHAKRAS

Traditionally there are seven or eight chakras; however, there are many more that exist. In terms of looking at an animal's energy block, it's best to concentrate on the seven best-known chakras. Here's a little glimpse of what they mean:

— The **first chakra**, or **root chakra**, is located in the region between the genitals and the anus and is associated with the color red. In humans and animals, the root chakra represents survival, instincts, and security. For humans, this sense of safety and security includes identification with our tribe, family, and social circles. When it comes to animals, it's their association with their pack, herd, pride, or flock. This holds true even as present families now have become multispecies. Human instincts get overruled by reason, but animals—predator and prey alike—have a keen sense of knowing about what's coming up behind them. It's imprinted onto them for survival, and these instincts are also associated with the immune system.

— The **second chakra**, or **sacral chakra**, is associated with the color orange. For both humans and animals, the sexual organs sit in this chakra, which represents sexual energy, emotion, and power. Interestingly enough, many dogs and cats have hip problems that can be traced back to when they were spayed or neutered.

— The **third chakra**, or **solar plexus**, is associated with the color yellow. For humans and animals, this chakra represents self-esteem, control, and career issues—this also is where digestion begins for both. Biochemistry can be thrown off by not fully expressing oneself or being misunderstood. So many horses have ill-fitting saddles in this region, thus blocking their true potential.

— The **fourth chakra**, or **heart chakra**, is associated with the color green. For humans and animals, this chakra is associated with devotion, compassion, and universal or unconditional love. Our most tender yet vital organs—the heart and lungs—are here. Again, this is an area of saddle soreness for horses. In addition, many dogs shoulder so much in a household that they get arthritis in this part of the spine.

UNDERSTANDING CHAKRAS, CONT'D.

— The **fifth chakra,** or **throat chakra,** is associated with the color blue. It represents self-expression, creativity, or spiritual expression. For humans and animals alike, some injury or blow to the system throws the biochemistry off, and the thyroid gets kooky. Many dogs have trauma to this part of their spine due to collars and yanking on their leashes.

— The **sixth chakra,** or **third eye,** is associated with the color indigo (violet or purple is sometimes mentioned as well). For humans and animals, this chakra is associated with intuition and perception. Many people have shut this area down and wouldn't recognize a telepathic message if they heard one, and they certainly aren't going to perceive their pets as intuitive or perceptive. Many animals are waiting for you to come home because they sense you from afar and are tuned in to this area before your car turns onto your street. They can also be tuned in to other energies around a house or a person.

— The **seventh chakra,** or **crown chakra,** is associated with the color white. For humans and animals alike, this chakra is about connection to the Divine or One Mind. Many animals have experienced trauma to the top of their head, and like humans with a head injury, their whole system is a bit "off." Craniosacral work is wonderful for reconnecting to the universe, in addition to the body. After a blow, this part of the body could throw all of the biochemistry, as well as the nervous system, out of alignment.

I've found that a fair number of dogs have aggression issues as a result of a head injury. They're completely disconnected in this area in order to escape the pain. In addition, they're short-tempered and quick to react because the alignment with their own bodies, and the whole universe around them, is so challenged.

We're part of animals' Divine connection, just as they're part of ours. If there's a poll (top-of-the-head) problem with your horse, it could be related to being disconnected from the right relationship.

As you look at where your animal companion has sustained an injury or has a medical condition, check if it's correlated with the physical locations of those chakras. Is it associated with any of the chakras' emotional components?

Energy Work

The laying on of hands goes back to the time of Christ and before. Whenever you practice this with intention, you can affect another person's energy. Just for starters, rub your hands together and then pull them apart slowly. See how far out they can go while still maintaining that *energy* or magnetism between them. With intention, this force can only have a positive healing outcome.

Laying your hands on an animal after a surgery can be calming, and doing so when an animal is scared has a soothing effect. Knowing that your animal is out of balance and laying your hands on the spine can actually morph the alignment right back where it's supposed to be. At the very least, the laying on of hands will relax the animal.

I went out to a barn to talk to a mare in Enumclaw, Washington. Her owner told me that she didn't know what was wrong. I got quiet and connected with the horse. After I'd made my notes, I just automatically put my hands on the area above the ovaries. The woman asked me why the horse was so upset. I didn't know anything about the family, but I told her that it was because the mare's person had completely disappeared and abandoned her. The woman said, "That would be my daughter. Since she left for college two years ago, she has abandoned all of us."

Both the horse and the woman were experiencing the abandonment. Then I asked if they were planning to breed the mare (who was confused about this). The woman said yes but that the horse hadn't come into heat in the two years since her daughter had left. The woman shed tears, and there was audible relief from the mare in the form of a

221

big sigh. We talked about what the woman could do with the horse if they weren't going to breed her.

When the mare was pulled out of the stall, she came into heat with a splash (I'm not kidding) before our very eyes. I personally think that it was a result of the combination of the woman and the horse releasing their shared sorrow and my hands over the ovaries relaxing her system.

There are many methods that don't require your hands, such as Reiki, ThetaHealing, and the Bioscalar Wave created by Dr. Valerie Hunt, just to name a few. I personally use the Bioscalar Wave, along with some other little techniques. I center myself and proceed through the animal's body—knowing the personality and/or physical complications, I go in and energetically balance the system, allowing it to get itself back on course. The body wants to survive, but sometimes a condition or "illness" has a strong hold on the animal.

Through energy work, you can reprogram the healthy tissue or the strongest organs to prevail over the condition. Whether you're a skilled energy worker or making it up as you go along, the most important things to remember are to hold a good intention and have no agenda. I know that sounds tricky: Intention but no agenda seems almost contradictory—but it's not. The right intention is for the highest good of all . . . no agenda means that you're not trying to save your pet's life if it's the animal's time to go.

Marianne and Hannah (Revisited)

Like animal communication, energy knows no time or space, so the recipient of healing doesn't have to be in the same room or even the same country. Marianne, the woman from Chapter 4 whose dog Hannah had Rocky Mountain spotted fever, went through so much trying to keep Hannah's immune system going strong. I might be anywhere in the country and get an e-mail from Marianne saying that the dog needed some help. I'd get quiet, connect with Hannah, and then be able to work on her from my present location. Moments later, I'd get a call from Marianne, who'd tell me, "Wow, we thought that this was the end, and then she just got up and trotted off!" This went on for years.

On one occasion I was actually at their house—most of our relationship had been via phone and e-mail—and I did some energy work on Hannah. She was receptive and lovely to work with. We went into a trance together. This time we were in so deep that it actually felt as if the air were turning into water, and suddenly it seemed as though Hannah were drowning. In this state, I pulled her up for air. After I was done, Marianne asked me what happened—she said that she could sense that we were in a very deep hypnotic state.

I replied, "Funny that you should say 'deep,'" and I proceeded to tell her what had happened. Larry, Marianne's husband, chimed in to say that Hannah was the only Lab on the planet who hated water and refused to swim. Marianne suggested that maybe Hannah had drowned in a past life.

About a month later, Marianne called and said, "Joan, you're not going to believe this, but Hannah jumped in the ocean today and swam and swam!"

My intention had been to go in and work on Hannah's immune system—and anything else that came up. Never in my wildest dreams would I have thought to go in and heal "water phobia" for an eight-year-old Lab. But after that, Hannah was a swimmer!

Shannon and Smooch

My friend Shannon called because her dog, Smooch, was in terrible shape after what most people (including Shannon, her vet, and other healers) concluded was the result of ingesting the herbicide Roundup Ready. The dog was in the hospital in Orlando on fluids. Shannon asked me to work on Smooch from where I was. I told her at the time what I tell everyone about an animal in such a critical state: "This may help the animal stay here and be healthier, but it could also make the crossing more blissful."

Although Shannon was distraught, she also knew that this was how it had to be. Prior to that night, if we did energy work on the dog, he had some immediate relief in the form of passing urine—so we all had a glimmer of hope that Smooch might stay here on Earth.

I ran the energy, and it was like floating through his system. When I got to the chakras, not only was I trying to give them a spin in a clockwise manner, I was also attempting to put the proper colors in place. All I could see was white—the most glorious white, as if somebody had a spotlight on them, reflecting them back up to me. I brought the energy in, but it felt as if it were falling back out. I was aware of somebody being very upset, as though Western medicine had failed the person. I thought that this was odd, and I kept trying to get it out of my head.

About five minutes later, the phone rang: It was Shannon in Orlando. She said that Smooch had crossed over a few minutes ago. She also mentioned that the vet had called her in hysterics, upset by how hard she'd tried to save him—and yet failed. We all had done the best we could, and Smooch had a glorious passing, so the vet really didn't "fail."

Traditional and Complementary Medicine

Energy work can be as simple as deciding that you want to change the vibes in your household or as complex as having psychic surgery. Either way, it's a powerful tool. Just as I believe that we're all animal communicators, I also think that we're all energy workers. Many energetic modalities had been around long before we were making diagnoses through blood work and fixing things with drugs. While this is considered "alternative" or "complementary" healing by Western medicine, I like to think of certain modalities and some energy work as the truly *traditional* medicine.

Having blood work run on your animal when its health is in question is important for two reasons: (1) It eases your mind, and (2) it's a quick way of getting to the root of the animal's dis-ease. But even the illness can have a deeper cause somewhere else, whether it's an emotional imbalance or exposure to toxins. There are plenty of ways to continue to handle the situation with both Western and traditional energetic medicine.

Then there are all those times when somebody calls me in because they think that their animal has a behavioral problem. More often than not, there's a definite block in the flow of energy within its skeletal system. By using energy medicine, you can find little things that are out of balance. Start by running your hands over the animal to establish a baseline of where the energy flows. When you have an intimate understanding of what it feels like on a good day, your hands may discover where the blocks are when things seem "off."

For example, if a so-called behavior problem springs up with your horse, try running your hands over its skeleton. You may find pockets of heat or coolness, or an area where the flow of energy just stops. It may not be time to invite the horse whisperer over to fix the behavior—it could simply be time for a chiropractic visit. Sometimes the horse whisperer is still necessary if the physiological situation gets etched in the muscle memory and the behavior continues. (I'll discuss releasing muscle memory in the next section.)

There's a time and a place for all Western medicine. What a miracle surgery, blood work, and antibiotics can be if they're necessary! However, sometimes the treatment from Western medicine costs too much in terms of side effects for these sensitive little creatures. Finding a holistic veterinarian who might treat your ailing animal with acupuncture, chiropractic, herbs, and other alternative modalities is really helpful. You *can* have the best of both worlds.

As you can see, there are many ways to read your animals and numerous energetic remedies for clearing their blocks. The energy work that I use and teach is a powerful tool for releasing trauma in their psyches as well as their cells. More advanced use would require spending some time at a reputable energy worker's seminar where you can get hands-on techniques. Otherwise, this is where other practitioners come into play. Finding someone to do this amazing work on your pet is a fantastic way to relieve the animal of its challenges.

Caroline Myss, a respected leader in the field of energy medicine, says, "Your biography becomes your biology." Behavioral and physiological challenges can become totally intertwined. As simple as it sounds, a good canine, feline, or equine massage therapist could release an emotional trauma *before* it turns into an unwanted behavior.

Muscle Memory

A very important aspect of healing past memories lies in the physical body. Not only can the body hang on to physical trauma, but it can inform the way we conduct ourselves from that point on. We've all seen some people let their chest cave in and their shoulders slump after a major heartbreak, or we've witnessed people and animals create other breakdowns in their physical bodies after injuring one limb and compensating with the other. An accident, an illness, or some other incident can create a pattern of energy in the body, whether it's scar tissue or a fear of loud cars. The body takes on the trauma and thereafter responds differently. And all of this contributes to cellular memory.

The term *cellular memory* means that even if you've forgotten the injury itself, the body hasn't—and the trauma is now lodged in your cells. Massage therapists for humans don't necessarily think of themselves as psychic, but the body they're working on will give explicit pictures of what sorts of accidents have happened to the client. In most cases, animals can let go of the trauma more readily than humans, as they don't hang on to issues in the subconscious in the way that we do.

Even though the memory can be long gone, animals hold themselves physically as if whatever injured or traumatized them is a continued threat. Take, for example, a dog that has been attacked by another dog. The victim could end up with *muscular armor,* an extra band of tissue that's so tense in the front end that it could be dragging along the rear. Or a dog that's aggressive could have an overly developed hind end in order to launch itself at another. Sometimes such dogs have had a prior head injury, and the cranial bones are pressing on them and creating the tension. In addition to the muscular strain, this could create emotional "on guard" behavior or physiological stress such that eventually the dog just reacts and goes into fight-or-flight mode if a dried leaf falls. There could ultimately be a drain on the adrenal glands.

Another scenario is continued protection of an injured area long after the pain is gone, which then becomes a compensation pattern. Let's say that a horse had a right-hind-leg injury and is then pulling along with the front left leg. So now even though it was the right hind leg that was initially hurt, the left shoulder carries the extra tension. The spine and hips get out of alignment, then the saddle doesn't fit, and so on. Because the tension will sneak around the body, it's very important to stay on top of injuries after the lameness appears to be gone; otherwise, you'll slowly notice the animal "communicating" a sense of malaise or aloofness—or worse, start acting cranky about things it used to love.

Become aware of where you hold the tension in your own body. If it's in your shoulders, put your attention there for a moment. See how fast the discomfort moves to another place in your body. Bodily strain is a very sneaky thing. There are physical and emotional reasons for the buildup in that particular area. Allow the tension to dissipate and see if you sense relief.

Sometimes riders will have an old injury that they're protecting. I've injured my right side several times, once while on one of my horses. Not only do that animal and I have a bit of unease now going around to the right, but I've created this pattern in my other horse. My right movement on *both* of them isn't as fluid. Try as I might to breathe into my right side, the damage has already been done. I now have to not only consciously open up my right side, but I have to micromanage the horses' right sides.

Many people who've had an experience where their dog was either attacked or *was* the attacker while on a leash have come to consciously walk their dog in such a way that the leash becomes the link to the memory. As another dog passes, the person tenses and the dog reacts.

In the animal field, nobody has done more to break up this pattern than Linda Tellington-Jones. She created her own circular "massage" system called TTouch. With this work, you're at the very least allowing the body to go into parasympathetic-nervous-system relaxing. While the sympathetic nervous system is involved in fight or flight, the parasympathetic nervous system is used to calm and regenerate. When you are able to get an animal into this state, healing can begin. The body wants to repair itself—it's built to live and thrive. You're also deepening the bond between you and the animal because of your intention, which increases the trust between you. In most cases, it really does change the physiological situation.

In Tellington-Jones's book *The Tellington TTouch* (with Sybil Taylor), she states:

> The circles of the TTouch seem to provide a way for this "cellular intelligence" common to all life to become communication, for the cells of one being to make a direct connection with the cells of another. It's as if the TTouch communicates across species barriers like a person-to-person call in which the same language is spoken although the callers are from different countries.
>
> Your circular "call" wakes up the cells of that other being, activating them to release stored memories of pain, "dis-ease," or the expectation of pain, and allowing them to "remember" their encoded potential for perfection.

Chiropractic, acupuncture, energy work, massage, hydrotherapy, homeopathic, Emotional Freedom Techniques, craniosacral therapy, vitamins, feng shui, hypnotherapy, energy enhancers such as Rife machines, and so on—all of these modalities were created to change the pattern. A deep-seated belief system, a memory that you're hanging on to for your pet, or a thought suggesting that it do the unthinkable still holds the animal to the behavior, yet the positive influence of these modalities can help improve the behavior and wellness of the animal. Change can occur with any of these support systems. You don't have to get your dog a lobotomy to stop him from digging!

Years ago, my horse and I had an accident and I broke my leg. I had surgery, a metal plate inserted, and the whole nine yards. Once the cast was off, I wanted to go back to jumping rope immediately. One morning when I tried it, it was so painful that I became very depressed. I didn't dare attempt it again for a very long time, and that brought me down further. One day I'd parked my car (I was in Los Angeles) and was walking down the street. I turned around by chance and saw a meter maid by the car. I *ran* back so fast and put money in the meter. As I continued walking again, I realized that I'd just run! Fantastic . . . I'd finally forgotten I was in pain.

A lot of times when a rider has had an accident or a person really can't let go of the picture of their darling, loving dog going for the throat of another animal, I suggest hypnotherapy just to relax the individual's mind around the event so that he or she can get back on the horse or the dog can still walk down the street. A hypnotherapist friend of mine, Pamela Shenk, says that what the mind believes, the body achieves—real or imagined. All of the preceding support systems would help the human as well. I've known people and their animals to get worked on by the same practitioner with great success.

Valuable Modalities

As much time as I've spent in muddy pastures talking to horses and mules or in sterile doggy day cares that smell of bleach, there's another variety of household I visit: that of the very spoiled pet. I've seen dogs with jewels and outfits that many *people* could only dream of affording. This is how some owners are expressing love. There are all different ways to do so, whether it's a pink and green dog dress or simply putting an old pillow on the ground for arthritic bones to lie on.

The list on the next page is another way to show caring, even if you don't have any physical or behavioral challenges to deal with—but the list is especially awesome to consult if you do encounter one. A lot of these modalities may even be *necessary* for old injuries or anxiety.

I think that all horses should get attention if they're being worked. Consider the direction of their spine (horizontal) versus ours (vertical). And then we hop on them and do ballet or jump or run through the woods. Many leg injuries wouldn't happen if the horses' spines were aligned. The same goes for other animals as well.

Many dogs, cats, and horses that are quick to react have cranial pressure. (The head isn't a single bone, but a *series* of them.) A slight head injury or funny landing can compress the vertebrae all the way up to the cranial bones, pushing them up and over one of the eyes, which then sees differently from the other one. You can easily tell that this is the case when a horse is spooked from one side and turns to look with the other eye, when a dog reacts too quickly to things that move by, or even when a cat darts out of the room for no apparent reason.

As I've mentioned a few times, aggressive dogs frequently have had a bad experience, and it's locked into their system. It can also be quite obvious that their cranial bones are pressing against the brain. However, there's a direct link between aggression and the thyroid being off, so get that tested first. Then consider the following types of treatment:

- Massage
- Acupuncture
- Acupressure
- Chiropractic
- Craniosacral therapy
- Energy work (such as Bioscalar Wave, Theta-Healing, and Reiki)
- Healing Touch
- TTouch
- Aromatherapy
- Magnets
- Laser therapy
- Rife machine
- Herbs
- Homeopathy
- Flower essences
- Hypnotherapy

When it comes to cancer, some of the various modalities mentioned aren't appropriate, and it's best to work with a holistic vet. Some practitioners won't do acupuncture but *will* treat with herbs. Many don't recommend massage, as they don't want any of the cancer cells to proliferate.

When a person has made a choice to do chemotherapy or radiation for their animal's condition, I always recommend an improved diet (depending on what the condition is) and building a better immune system so that the body has a chance to thrive in health and thus ask the cancer cells to move on out. The animal's system must have been out of balance to create the illness in the first place, and then the foreign substance such as chemotherapy or radiation can really send it out of whack. Regardless of the choices made around treatment, building up the immune system is necessary.

I'm very passionate about nutrition because I've lost two horses to mistakes in feeding—Pet One, my soulmate horse; and three years later, her son, Pony Boy. I've seen thousands of animals needlessly struggle with illnesses and behavioral situations that could have been eliminated through a better understanding of diet or over-vaccination. I strongly urge you to learn as much as you can about food, vaccines, and which alternative-healing methods are available to you. More up-to-date information on nutrition, health, healing modalities, and practitioners can be obtained on my Website: **www .joanranquet.com.**

May you and your animal family be blessed with being happy, healthy, safe, and sound . . . living long, full, active lives. Whenever you get a chance, be kind to Mother Earth and thank her for housing us—she could use your prayers.

True humanness consists of a continuous series of tiny acts executed with absolute sincerity and largeness of heart.
— Sai Baba

❖ Afterword ❖

*I like pigs. Dogs look up to men, cats look
down on them, but pigs just treat us as equals.*
— Winston Churchill

Only a few things are actually required for animal-communication work:

- Finding a place within or having the ability to get quiet (if you aren't a quiet-sitting yogi type, at least learn how to cut out the chatter)

- Having an open heart and compassion

- Learning to trust yourself

- Having the willingness to look through the lens of another

- Practicing all of the above

Learning and developing this work may enable someone out there to help all the animals in the zoo as well as all nonverbal humans . . . communicate better, make an anxiety-ridden dog feel better while you're at work, allow you to win the Kentucky Derby, and assist you in connecting more deeply with your cat.

It's all important. Animal communication is well worth the effort. Once you get past the learning curve, it becomes a state of being. It's just a part of the labyrinth of coexistence—which can be a very powerful and magical place to be!

Working with People

One of the most common questions I'm asked is: "Do the same techniques work with people?" Yes. However, in general I choose not to work with people. I've done so in very particular situations, and I'll share more about that in a moment. The biggest reason why I don't, though, is that I love animals and am constantly amazed by what they have to teach and the simplicity with which their message comes through. Another reason why is that there are many, many others who do far greater things in that capacity than I could ever do. Last, people are messy! Sifting through human "stuff" just from an animal's perspective is enough for me, thank you very much!

I will, however, work with nonverbal humans— that is, babies and people who have no ability to communicate. Little Bit Therapeutic Riding Center in the Seattle area has used me to work with nonverbal kids. I started out just as their animal communicator, helping their horses when they were having challenges in the therapeutic-horseback-riding program, and then the work moved to nonverbal children.

One very bold physical therapist, Debbie, used my skills for a few kids, starting with Stephen. Debbie knew that Stephen was going through something. However, she was entirely too close to the situation to identify what it was.

Stephen had been born with his umbilical cord wrapped around his neck. At the time I met him, he was 13 years old, and his hormones would, or should, have been kicking in. Many people suspected that the hormonal shift was the cause of his seeming discomfort in life. While it may have fueled some of his distress, Debbie had a sense that something more than hormones was disturbing Stephen—she just couldn't pinpoint what it was.

Stephen's mother didn't necessarily believe in animal communication or telepathy, so we introduced it very casually during one of his riding sessions. Stephen was lifted onto his favorite horse, a Fjord pony, for his therapy. A Fjord pony has a very flat back, perfect for therapeutic-riding work, particularly for people with no control over or use of their limbs. Not only that, this noble animal loved his job: He lived to make children such as Stephen feel safe, loved, and dignified.

We slowly walked around the arena. Stephen was attended on either side by assistants and was led by a volunteer. Debbie continued her physical manipulations to stimulate his body. I walked alongside and mentally started to tune in to him. I have my own way of slipping into an animal's world, so this was a true challenge; I thought I'd start by considering how I'd talk to a typical kid. At the same time, I needed verifiable information so that I wasn't making assumptions about him and reporting my opinion.

I asked him what kind of work his dad did. In my head, I received the picture of a hardworking man and heard the word *engineer.* As we walked past Stephen's mother, I asked if her husband was an engineer. Startled, she almost yelled, "Yes!"—the subtext being: *How did you know?* The minutest smile glimmered on the kid's face for a second.

While continuing down the long side of the arena, Stephen and I maintained the connection we'd established. Like an animal I'm connecting to, I asked him mentally what he liked to do. He flashed me a picture of an airplane and a computer.

As we passed his mother again, I asked if he'd been flying recently. Now she seemed annoyed, responding, "We just went to San Francisco." Slowly his mother revealed that he loved the flight because he had a window seat. Also, she confirmed that Stephen was fascinated by computers.

All righty—now we were talking. What Stephen eventually revealed was that he had recently changed classes and that was what was upsetting him, bringing up insecurity about not knowing people in this new environment. He was depressed because for years he'd felt comfortable with the classmates who knew him.

His mother confirmed that he had indeed changed classes. She knew now that she needed to talk to his teachers about making sure he felt more included. It proved helpful enough to Stephen's mother that they continued to use my services.

In fact, years later his mother requested my help again, as it was clear that Stephen was physically very uncomfortable. What we all discovered was that a piece of equipment that had been inserted to keep his bodily functions going was creating the discomfort. He'd had a growth spurt, and now that piece of equipment was pinching him. They were able to surgically move the piece in such a way that he regained his former comfort level.

Our Evolving World

There's another place for which this work is very urgently needed: creating better cohabitation with all life here on planet Earth.

There's so much to examine—the emotional, spiritual, mental, symbolic, and literal components; as well as the socioeconomics, the science, and the energetics of it all (not to mention questions of political, spiritual, and environmental correctness). All of those issues bear on the one underlying question: *As we evolve, where are we going?* When it comes to animals, our friends at home are simply a microcosm or metaphor for that which is housed here by Mother Earth. We can't forget the question of what happens to all animals with respect to geographical or environmental concerns.

With brains continuing to develop and lifestyles for all beings intensifying, evolution is really hard upon us, and our future is at stake. It has taken us 2,000 years to get hybrid cars and watch a movie while flying through the air. Earth's giant population has created so many fantastic minds at work, facilitating spectacular engineering feats with respect to spaceships, unbelievable skylines, bridges, and even bras! People are creating things that generate "effortlessness" and compress time for us, including but not limited to electronic communication available for transmission within seconds. Evolution is now in hyperspeed.

Sadly, the consequences of having that much "ease" is that we've forgotten the simplicity of connection. We've taken away the steps that keep us focused, as in the proverb "Chop wood, carry water." We're easily distracted, as we're bombarded with so many images and collective thoughts and feelings in a great Ping-Pong game around us. What will this look like for humanity, animals, and the planet down the road?

Our impact on the planet is epic. Mother Earth is home to a multitude of species. What does that have to do with animal communication? *Everything.* As Earth gives us this home and we keep expanding and encroaching upon the natural existence of other species, we're faced with many challenges.

While in Seattle over the holidays, I saw an article about tests that were being conducted on how the overuse of cinnamon and vanilla in holiday cooking would eventually result in those seasonings ending up in Puget Sound. Researchers pondered how this would affect the salmon. I ask, *What about the rest—the plankton and the water itself?*

But how do we approach this dilemma? Animals in the wild have a different reality base than those in our homes, meaning that part of the evolution of the minute could look like a dog, a cat, an exotic bird, a few fish, and even some reptiles living in our homes. Examining that more deeply, we can actually see the sophistication and in-depth understanding they have of our everyday life. I've even had turtles—Olga and Misha—that listened to what I was saying. When Olga died, we all mourned her death along with Misha. While they looked prehistoric, these two beings melded perfectly into a modern lifestyle.

Your dog may not specifically understand that Aunt Mabel in Pennsylvania has cancer, but it comprehends that you're worried about the health of a family member and that a certain amount of your energy is being taken away from the household while you address your concerns. And some animals may even "get" that Aunt Mabel is ill. But a moose in Yellowstone wouldn't.

The reality is that we're faced with more and more images, feelings, and thoughts—our senses are on overload and are only speeding up. As our lives get more and more complicated, so will those of our animal companions. Additionally, we get further and further away from that moose in Yellowstone. All the while, we're upsetting an existence that had its own natural balance.

As we race down the evolutionary track and our takeover of Mother Nature becomes imminent, will we be sleeping with cougars and caging peregrine falcons? It's a quandary. Communication with such creatures is more of a struggle, as we have to slow down our thought process and understand that their needs are more survival oriented. How a wild animal communicates is going to be vastly different from how a Pomeranian in a New York penthouse vying for more attention does so.

Animals are with us . . . they are among us. In Los Angeles, I was told of a woman in the Hollywood Hills who one morning found a coyote asleep in her lawn chair. When she yelled, "Shoo!" trying to scare it off the chair and out of her yard, it just yawned, stretched each of its legs, and then with a final flex, hopped off the chair and casually trotted away.

We have to start at home and then branch out. Wolves waiting for leftovers outside our caves and by campsites during the Stone Age have resulted in dogs sleeping in bed with us. When we perfect the art of communication in the home, we have to learn a way to negotiate with the wild; otherwise, we'll continue to have unwanted encounters between joggers and cougars—and worse. We need to learn to listen . . . and think about that moose in Yellowstone.

Hurricane Katrina passed over south Florida before making its devastating landfall in Louisiana and Mississippi. The day it passed over Fort Lauderdale, the bird of a friend of mine there repeated, "Uh-oh, uh-oh, uh-oh." That particular hurricane only had a mild brush with Fort Lauderdale, but the year before Hurricanes Frances and Jeanne did more damage. The impact of another storm wasn't lost on that bird. Hurricane Katrina, with its ghastly force, was known to it, even though it had a loving life in a suburban home. There are many lessons to be learned by the instincts that have (thankfully) not yet been "domesticated" out of animals.

Listening starts at home. And in order to listen to *them,* we have to start by listening to ourselves and seeing what kind of messages we're sending—then we can make them better. From this set point of harmony, we can go outside and help our neighbor. Soon enough, that neighbor may be a brown bear!

Thank you for reading this book. The more we focus on this type of work and contemplate these questions of evolution, the more we can all be part of a community of intention and together leave the earth better off than we found it.

— **Joan Ranquet**

❖ Acknowledgments ❖

I have been very lucky to have this work be my life's path. Every single animal that has come my way—and their person—has truly blessed me. It's been a true act of grace. While most of my stories have focused on the dog, cat, bird, and horse culture, I want to mention that I have talked to many ferrets, guinea pigs, ducks, chickens, mice, rats, llamas, emus, monkeys, raptors, mules, turtles, tortoises, iguanas . . . and the list goes on.

The other thing that has been a blessing is the people I get to work with. Having a community is so helpful in order to really be of assistance to the animals. Wherever two or more are gathered. . . .

I am constantly exchanging notes with Carol Walker in the Seattle area, who is an awesome human psychic, medical intuitive, healer, and acupuncturist. Another acupuncturist, Audrey Temelini, in Charleston, was in school in Los Angeles years ago when I was there, and she was generous with each tidbit of knowledge she acquired.

I have learned a lot from the owners and managers of various doggy day cares that I've been fortunate enough to work at, like Chateau Marmutt in Los Angeles, Hounds on the Hill in Denver, and Central Bark in Fort Lauderdale.

I've also taught workshops there. Pet Lover's Central has Jamie at the helm, taking in dogs at her rescue. Terri Desnica at Hounds on the Hill is also a great dog trainer, and I've picked her brain. Years ago I used to pick the brain of Jeff Tinsley—another great dog trainer out of Seattle.

Chiropractor and nutrition expert Regan Golob and I have managed to land in the same town to work on animals together in many cities and rural areas. When it comes to nutrition, Judy Sinner Gold, executive director of Dynamite specialty products—a company for which I'm a distributor—cheerfully answers any silly questions I have.

When I was in Denver, I was lucky to have wonderful friendships and working associations. Dr. Turie Norman, a holistic vet, taught me a lot about food. I continue to get her assistance with Bach flower remedies. Also, chiropractors Drs. Debbie O'Reilly and Susan Crawford and I shared many clients and much knowledge. We still exchange information and send clients each other's way.

And of course, horse trainers—I love finding trainers who put the animal first. Together with both Christina Drake, a dressage trainer in the Seattle area, and Laura Rising, a three-day-event trainer, we've been able to really turn some horses around. And Chris Bennings in south Florida and I have gone to many barns together and helped some horses and their people. He also has helped both of *my* horses tremendously, as well as my own riding ability.

I've watched friends from all different careers make their way into the animal world, cashing in a corporate job to become a pet sitter or massage therapist. One friend, Ellen Fitzgerald, went from business accounting to saddle fitting, and I still get to pick her brain.

It's important to be able to exchange notes with others. We can get very myopic in our own world. Someone can come along and blow the doors open—and wow, there's a whole new perspective.

I also have a strong support system in my family: my dad, Mary, Faith, Mike, my aunt Barb, and my cousin Neilia . . . and friends who have been guiding of course include Robin.

I also wouldn't have gotten this done without the Barn Girls, who cheerfully took shifts feeding Pony Boy—Jenni, Judy, and Kelly. Of course, if Frank hadn't made me go to the barn after Kubla died, this story wouldn't have gotten started.

One of my favorite communities where I still work when I'm in Denver is the Twelfth House bookstore. Even though this New Age bookstore isn't animal related, all the other readers there are fabulous psychics, and we share our human experience. And if it weren't for Mark Husson, the owner there and the author of *Mark's Power Peek*, this book wouldn't be here.

❖ Resources ❖

Books

Foods Pets Die For, by Ann N. Martin

Natural Nutrition for Dogs and Cats, by Kymythy R. Schultze

Dr. Pitcairn's Complete Guide to Natural Health for Dogs & Cats, by Richard H. Pitcairn, D.V.M., Ph.D., and Susan Hubble Pitcairn

The Nature of Animal Healing, by Martin Goldstein, D.V.M.

Homeopathic Care for Cats and Dogs, by Don Hamilton, D.V.M.

The Encyclopedia of Natural Pet Care, by C.J. Puotinen

Animal-Meat Sources

Oma's Pride (**www.omaspride.com**)

Nature's Variety (**www.naturesvariety.com**)

Websites

On my Website, I have information
about supplements and products I carry—go to:
www.joanranquet.com.

For full range of Dynamic products, visit:
www.dynamitemarketing.com.

❖ About the Author ❖

Animal communicator **Joan Ranquet** has used telepathic communication in an innovative way for pet guardians, breeders, trainers, and health-care practitioners to get new information that leads to understanding an animal's problems and needs. Joan has acted as a translator for healing human/animal relations, solving behavior problems, isolating the discomfort of illnesses, easing the various stages of crossing over, and finding lost pets. She also uses energy work and/or bodywork to alleviate pain and teaches beginning and advanced animal communication.

Website: **www.joanranquet.com**

We hope you enjoyed this Hay House book. If you'd like to receive our online catalog featuring additional information on Hay House books and products, or if you'd like to find out more about the Hay Foundation, please contact:

Hay House, Inc., P.O. Box 5100, Carlsbad, CA 92018-5100
(760) 431-7695 or (800) 654-5126
(760) 431-6948 (fax) or (800) 650-5115 (fax)
www.hayhouse.com® • www.hayfoundation.org

Published in Australia by: Hay House Australia Pty. Ltd.,
18/36 Ralph St., Alexandria NSW 2015
Phone: 612-9669-4299 • *Fax:* 612-9669-4144
www.hayhouse.com.au

Published in the United Kingdom by: Hay House UK, Ltd.,
The Sixth Floor, Watson House, 54 Baker Street, London W1U 7BU
Phone: +44 (0)20 3927 7290 • *Fax:* +44 (0)20 3927 7291
www.hayhouse.co.uk

Published in India by: Hay House Publishers India,
Muskaan Complex, Plot No. 3, B-2, Vasant Kunj, New Delhi 110 070
Phone: 91-11-4176-1620 • *Fax:* 91-11-4176-1630
www.hayhouse.co.in

Access New Knowledge.
Anytime. Anywhere.

Learn and evolve at your own pace
with the world's leading experts.

www.hayhouseU.com

Printed in the United States
By Bookmasters